♦The Alchemy of Wealth♦

Kim & Terry,
Change the way
you look at things
and the things you
look at change!

[signature]

♦The Alchemy of Wealth♦

A review of Wallace Wattles 1910 classic

The Science of Getting Rich

Written by Wallace Wattles

John Dessauer

dessauer PUBLISHING™

www.JohnDessauer.com

To contact the author, please visit www.JohnDessauer.com

Library of Congress Cataloging-in-Publication Data is available upon request.
2009900611

ISBN-13: 978-0-615-27478-2
ISBN-10: 0-615-27478-2

Dessauer Publishing
130 North West Street | Crown Point, IN 46307
P- (866) 977-1515 | F-(219) 226-9460
www.JohnDessauer.com

Cover design by Michael A.C. Rebey
Interior design and formatting by Kristin Hansen

Contents

Foreword

Webster defines **al•che•my** [al-**k*uh*-mee**] as, "any magical power or process of transmuting a common substance, usually of little value, into a substance of great value." In *The Alchemy of Wealth*, John Dessauer does exactly that: He shows you the way that you, the reader, can create magic by developing a "process." That process can then take something of little value and turn it into WEALTH, which, of course, is something of great value.

John Dessauer (Johnny "D," as his friends and fans call him) has indeed created that alchemy in his own life: He took his chosen career path earlier in life, which was producing unsatisfactory results ("something of little value"), and turned himself magically into a wildly successful, real-estate-investing machine ("something of great value"). In fact, that "process" created colossal wealth for John Dessauer! Now, his personal experience is offered to serve as a marvelous inspiration to anyone who will take the time to consume this book.

I know from our professional relationship that Johnny "D" truly walks the walk and talks the talk of someone who has faced the precise challenges that occur in every journey to

WEALTH. The question remains, "Was it really magical, as Webster suggests; or was it just part of a simple 'process'?" **Only you** can be the judge of that! In my mind, that begs the question, "Would it be something truly magical if you took your existing life and created great WEALTH from that? I would tend to think that most of you reading this foreword would have to respond, "YES, it is unquestionably magical!"

For some reason, WEALTH creation seems to be a mystery to those who have been in pursuit of that most of their lives, yet have had wealth elude them. Most of the wealth-seekers I have encountered, who actually have remained unsuccessful in creating wealth, cannot, for the life of them, understand the reason why they themselves have failed in this arena, nor are they able to identify that which differentiates the successful upper echelon of those who achieve great wealth from those who have failed, like themselves, at realizing their own dreams of inestimable riches.

For most of these with failed attempts, it was not about lack of intelligence! Certainly, we all know those WITHOUT extraordinary intelligence who often have been enormously successful in attaining great WEALTH. I find that most of those in pursuit of WEALTH believe that attaining a high level of riches is not even about possessing special talent, since many of those who failed already also possess great talents. To most, it does not even seem to be about timing and trends, family background or opportunity. In fact, many of the people whom I have interviewed (and for whom WEALTH has escaped them personally) actually already possess several of the aforementioned blessings.

So what is it that we need in order to create real and sustainable WEALTH? **The answer is in this book!**

John Dessauer has accomplished an amazing feat by leveraging his personal experiences, sage advice of great mentors and a vast amount of wisdom from previous reading and study in an attempt to influence sincere wealth-seekers to discover for themselves a permanent, WEALTH-CREATION solution. In fact, *The Alchemy of Wealth* is a wonderful annotation to one of my favorite books, *The Science of Getting Rich* by the New-Thought-Movement writer Wallace D. Wattles. *The Science of Getting Rich* was originally published in 1910. That's correct -- almost 100 years ago! It is still in print, today. Along with *Think and Grow Rich*, Wattles' book was one of my greatest, pivotal influences in my successful, personal quest to attain great WEALTH!

John Dessauer has taken an age-old, mind-set science and applied it to the modern day. His contemporary thinking (described in unique half-chapters) can be applied, immediately! Surprisingly, nothing additional is required! ALL YOU HAVE TO DO IS READ THE ENTIRE BOOK AND APPLY ITS PRECEPTS! Could it be that simple?

When you carefully study *The Alchemy of Wealth*, you will discover for yourself that which many successful "wealth alchemists" already know! Simply put, WEALTH CREATION is a process that begins in your mind and extends to your attitude. Yes, WEALTH CREATION really IS a process of "transmuting a common substance, usually of little value, into a substance of great value." That is the TRUE Alchemy of Wealth! That is yours for discovering by reading John Dessauer's great chef d'oeuvre!

Enjoy the process!

-Jim Piccolo

Friend, Mentor, Entrepreneur and Philanthropist

Preface

THIS BOOK IS PRAGMATICAL, NOT philosophical; a practical manual, not a treatise upon theories. It is intended for the men and women whose most pressing need is for money, who wish to get rich first, and philosophize afterward. It is for those who have, so far, found neither the time, the means, nor the opportunity to go deeply into the study of metaphysics, but who want results and who are willing to take the conclusions of science as a basis for action, without going into all the processes by which those conclusions were reached.

It is expected that the reader will take the fundamental statements upon faith, just as he would take statements concerning a law of electrical action if they were promulgated by a Marconi or an Edison; and, taking the statements upon faith, that he will prove their truth by acting upon them without fear or hesitation. Every man or woman who does this will certainly get rich; for the science herein applied is of those who wish to investigate philosophical theories and so secure a logical basis for faith, I will here cite certain authorities.

The monistic theory of the universe- the theory that One is All, and that All is One; that one Substance manifests itself as the seeming many elements of the material world—is of Hindu origin, and has been gradually winning its way into the thought of the Western world for two hundred years. It is the foundation of all the Oriental philosophies, and those of Descartes, Spinoza, Leibnitz, Schopenhauer, Hegel, and Emerson.

The reader who would dig to the philosophical foundations of this is advised to read Hegel and Emerson for himself.

In writing this book I have sacrificed all other considerations to plainness and simplicity of style, so that all might understand. The plan of action laid down herein was deduced from the conclusions of philosophy; it has been thoroughly tested, and bears the supreme test of practical experiment; it works. If you wish to know how the conclusions were arrived at, read the writings of authors mentioned above; and if you wish to reap the fruits of their philosophies in actual practice, read this book and do exactly as it tells you to do.

THE AUTHOR

Preface ½

I HAVE BEEN ABSOLUTELY EXCITED TO GET involved in writing a book about the *Science of Getting Rich* for such a long time. The author, Wallace Wattles, wrote the original book in 1910. I can just imagine the thought of wealth then and how some greats such as Andrew Carnegie and Marshall Field gave people a new hope to fulfill all of the dreams that people had as the industrial revolution hit with full force.

I also know that wealth is a science. My background, from an education standpoint, may fit perfectly with this book. In undergraduate school, I double majored in Biology and Business Administration. Science and business, it couldn't be a better combination to talk about this most famous book that was written such a long time ago. The title alone, *The Science of Getting Rich* implies that science and all of its rules play a part in getting rich! Wallace Wattles was right!

How can science play a part in getting rich? Well for one, I know that science is exact. It has a set of rules that are to be followed. It has been what has explained everything from how our universe was created to how humans are able to destroy the planet. How does that apply to getting rich? Well all of science can begin with a certain creation, a creation that acts as a beginning of a series of events. Those events, when rolled out, will allow you to accomplish, achieve and acquire all that you need and want in your life. It will even make you rich!

It can't be that simple though or can it? I am a believer in what *The Science of Getting Rich* has to say. It's a manual of sorts. It is a book that should be kept very close to the reader's heart. If you truly create something in your mind and you focus enough, you will start the very process that will produce physically what you created in your mind.

Why *The Alchemy of Wealth*? Historically, "alchemy" was originally known as a science that takes obscure, common metals (lead) and changes them into gold. Such a transformation would mean quite a deal more than just the physical elemental change.

The physical transformation meant power and possibly the opportunity of eternal life. The debate about eternal life, I will leave possibly for a book I may write in the future. However, alchemy does have to do with life; the betterment of it.

This subject of alchemy is not to be taken as the occult or supernatural. Alchemy within the context of this book is to be used in the idea of change and advancement in life. I hope you can use the information to make a dramatic future for yourself and your family.

Each chapter of *The Alchemy of Wealth* is a text book to have you take action and get you rich! I will be giving you my thoughts on Wallace Wattles' classic and also giving you some insight as to what he said in 1910 applies to us today. We will go through Wallace Wattles chapter first and then I will give you my chapter of thoughts and how it applies today. My chapters will be listed as ½ chapters to distinguish between the two. *The Science of Getting Rich*, may be one of the most important reads of a person's life. Enjoy the book and if you do exactly what it says you to will become a scientist of wealth! Enjoy!

Acknowledgements

IN MY FIRST BOOK, *REAL ESTATE H2O*, ONE of the things that I was most proud of was of the dedication that I had put at the beginning. This time, I would like to be more specific. The following are in no order of importance.

I have so many people to thank, specifically, my staff at The Dessauer Group. Kristin Hansen (Dessauer Publishing/Media); we couldn't create like we do without you! Carla Heminger, Ronda Dessauer, Jenni Pause and Lolly Lones; I couldn't do what I do without all of your support! I know all of you put in a tremendous amount of time to make sure everything we do runs smoothly and for that I thank you! What we do could not be possible if it was not for all of your efforts.

I would also like to thank the mentors that I have had in my career as a speaker, writer and radio show host. Including, but not limited to John Childers, Frank McKinney, Jim Piccolo, Nouveau Riche staff, Lee Michaels, Brian O'Connell, Robert Allen, EWI staff, Mark Victor Hansen, Mark Kohler, David Dweck and last, but not least, Tory and Mary Kay Prasco.

I would also like to thank my family. As long as I have been on the journey as an entrepreneur, I have asked you to all sacrifice and to share the vision that I have in my mind. Sometimes that is where the challenge comes into play. Shared visions are difficult to keep everyone on the same page.

Jordan and Payton, I would especially like to thank you for the inspiration you give me every day. I write in part because of the permanent messages that I can leave for you and future generations. I trust that you will live the lessons that you can learn in my books. Thank you both for who you are!

Thank you again, and I love you all! (Now Lets have some fun!)

Congratulations on what you are about to achieve!

CHAPTER ONE

♦THE RIGHT TO BE RICH♦

WHATEVER MAY BE SAID IN PRAISE OF poverty, the fact remains that it is not possible to live a really complete or successful life unless one is rich. No man can rise to his greatest possible height in talent or soul development unless he has plenty of money; for to unfold the soul and to develop talent he must have many things to use, and he cannot have these things unless he has money to buy them with.

A man develops in mind, soul, and body by making use of things, and society is so organized that man must have money in order to become the possessor of things; therefore, the basis of all advancement for man must be the science of getting rich.

The object of all life is development; and everything that lives has an inalienable right to all the development it is capable of attaining.

Man's right to life means his right to have the free and unrestricted use of all the things which may be necessary to his fullest mental, spiritual, and physical unfoldment; or, in other words, his right to be rich.

In this book, I shall not speak of riches in a figurative way; to be really rich does not mean to be satisfied or contented with a little. No man ought to be satisfied with a little if he is capable of using and enjoying more. The purpose of Nature is the advancement and unfoldment of life; and every man should have all that can contribute to the power; elegance, beauty, and richness of life, to be content with less is sinful.

The man who owns all he wants for the living of all the life he is capable of living is rich; and no man who has not plenty of money can have all he wants. Life has advanced so far, and become so complex, that even the most ordinary man or woman requires a great amount of wealth in order to live in a manner that even approaches completeness. Every person naturally wants to become all that they are capable of becoming; this desire to realize innate possibilities is inherent in human nature; we cannot help wanting to be all that we can be. Success in life is becoming what you want to be; you can become what you want to be only by making use of things, and you can have the free use of things only as you become rich enough to buy them. To understand the science of getting rich is therefore the most essential of all knowledge.

There is nothing wrong in wanting to get rich. The desire for riches is really the desire for a richer, fuller, and more abundant life; and that desire is praiseworthy. The man who does not desire to live more abundantly is abnormal, and so the man who does not desire to have money enough to buy all he wants is abnormal.

There are three motives for which we live; we live for the body, we live for the mind, we live for the soul. No one of those is better or holier that the other; all are alike desirable, and no one of the three—body, mind, or soul—can live fully if either of the others is cut short of full life and expression. It is not right or noble to live only for the soul and deny the mind or body; and it is wrong to live for the intellect and deny body or soul.

We are all acquainted with the loathsome consequence of living for the body and denying both mind and soul; and we see that *real* life means the complete expression of all that man can give forth through body, mind, and soul. Whatever he can say, no man can be really happy or satisfied unless his body is living fully in every function, and unless the same is true of his mind and his soul. Wherever there is unexpressed possibility, or function not performed, there is unsatisfied desire. Desire is possibility seeking expression, or function seeking performance.

Man cannot live fully in body without good food, comfortable clothing, and warm shelter; and without freedom from excessive toil. Rest and recreation are also necessary to his physical life.

He cannot live fully in mind without books and time to study them, without opportunity for travel and observation, or without intellectual companionship.

To live fully in mind he must have intellectual recreations, and must surround himself with all the objects of art and beauty he is capable of using and appreciating.

To life fully in soul, man must have love; and love is denied expression by poverty.

A man's highest happiness is found in the bestowal of benefits on those he loves; love finds its most natural and spontaneous expression in giving. The man who had nothing to give cannot fill his place as a husband or father, as a citizen, or as a man. It is in the use of material things that a man finds full life for his body, develops his mind, and unfolds his soul. It is therefore of supreme importance to him that he should be rich.

It is perfectly right that you should desire to be rich; if you are a normal man or woman you cannot help doing so. It is perfectly right that you should give your best attention to the Science of Getting Rich, for it is the noblest and most necessary of all studies. If you neglect this study, you are derelict in your duty to yourself, to God, and to humanity; for you can render to God and humanity no greater service than to make the most of yourself.

CHAPTER ONE ½

THE FIRST CHAPTER OF THIS BOOK removes the shackles of the idea of getting rich. We have heard it throughout our lives, that there is something about wealth that is evil and that money and having money is bad. The idea that we have the right to be rich is something that should be a universal fact.

The sentence, "the object of all life is development" was very big for me. The object of all life is development. Wow, when I look back at all of the training that I have had in biology labs and concepts, it all points to one thing, development (of life). If you look at the locomotion of animals and the way that they consume energy, it is for the supreme purpose to develop as a species. They do small things for the main objective of giving a better chance to themselves and their offspring to develop and make their species stronger.

Develop, advance and make progress. Going from point A to point B. We are all part of this thing called life and it is our right to use all and any resources of the universe to make that happen. Think about that idea alone. We can use anything in the universe to advance ourselves as an individual, which will advance our society. Our resources are staggering. Actually, our resources are limitless. That one idea has allowed me to eliminate the word "can't" from my vocabulary.

To have our bodies, mind and soul be present together, as a fine tuned engine, so that we can achieve our destiny is something of beauty. A destiny that we create within our own mind is the magic or should I say miracle of life. It is the true balance that we all strive for. It is the comfort in which we look for when doing certain things such as meditation or yoga. We all strive for a higher power of guidance throughout our lives.

This creation of things in our mind already makes us rich and extremely powerful. The idea of awareness and self-awareness is what separates us from many of the other animals that we share and have shared this planet with. If we are aware of our power and choose not to use it, we are no better than a rock. However, we should choose to use our powers to provide a rich life for ourselves, where we can not only live, dance and admire, but love, that's when man truly understands the ideas of wealth. That's when we are one with our creator.

A fulfilled life is one with a purpose, a life that has a mission. We know that is a way to better the chances of improving who we are and how we develop. To discover the concept that we can conceive an idea in our minds that will make our cup overflow with opportunities to satisfy our thirst for success.

Unfortunately, that is under minded by a lot of areas of society today. For example, the news, religious organizations and our education system, to name a few.

Understand also, that achieving will also allow you to advance the spirit of who we are as a species. That spirit is giving. Towards the end of the chapter Wallace Wattles writes: The man who has nothing to give cannot fill his place as a husband or father, as a citizen, or as a man. Learn to give with your wealth. Serve with giving not only though money but also time and knowledge. Stay busy with your mission in life and you will find that you do not have time to involve negativity; something that stops most people from becoming rich.

Are you ready to become rich?

CHAPTER TWO

♦THERE IS A SCIENCE OF GETTING RICH♦

THERE IS A SCIENCE OF GETTING RICH, and it is an exact science like algebra or arithmetic. There are certain laws which govern the process of acquiring riches; once these laws are learned and obeyed by any man, he will get rich with mathematical certainty.

The ownership of money and property comes as a result of doing things in a Certain Way; those do things in this Certain Way, whether on purpose or accidentally, get rich; while those who do not do things in this Certain Way, no matter how hard they work or how able they are, remain poor.

It is natural law that like causes always produce like effects; and therefore, any man or woman who learns to do things in this Certain Way will infallibly get rich.

That the above statement is true is shown by the following facts:

Getting rich is not a matter of environment, for, if it were, all the people in certain neighborhoods would become wealthy; the people of one city would all be poor; or the inhabitants of one state would roll in wealth, while those of an adjoining state would be in poverty.

But everywhere we see rich and poor living side by side, in the same environment, and often engaged in the same vocations. When two men are in the same locality, and in the same business, and one gets rich while the other remains poor, it shows that getting rich is not, primarily, a matter of environment. Some environments may be more favorable than others, but when two men in the same business are in the same neighborhood, and one gets rich while the other fails, it indicates that getting rich is the result of doing things in a Certain Way.

And further, the ability to do things in this Certain Way is not due solely to the possession of talent, for many people who have great talent remain poor, while other who have very little talent get rich.

Studying the people who have gotten rich, we find that they are an average lot in all respects, having no greater talents and abilities than other men. It is evident that they do not get rich because they possess talents and abilities that other men have not, but because they happen to do things in a Certain Way.

Getting rich is not the result of saving, or "thrift;" many very penurious people are poor, while free spenders often get rich.

Nor is getting rich due to doing things which others fail to do; for two men in the same business often do almost exactly the same things, and one gets rich while the other remains poor or becomes bankrupt.

From all these things, we must come to the conclusion that getting rich is the result of doing things in a Certain Way.

If getting rich is the result of doing things in a Certain Way, and if like cause always produce like effects, then any man or woman who can do things in that way can become rich, and the whole matter is brought within the domain of exact science.

The question arises here, whether this Certain Way may not be so difficult that only a few may follow it. This cannot be true, as we have seen, so far as natural ability is concerned. Talented people get rich, and blockheads get rich; intellectually brilliant people get rich, and very stupid people get rich; physically strong people get rich, and weak and sickly people get rich.

Some degree of ability to think and understand is, of course, essential, but insofar natural ability is concerned, any man or woman who has sense enough to read and understand these words can certainly get rich.

Also, we have seen that it is not a matter of environment. Location counts for something; one would not go to the heard of the Sahara and expect to do successful business.

Getting rich involves the necessity of dealing with men, and of being where there are people to deal with; and if these people are inclined to deal in the way you want to deal, so much the better. But that is about as far as environment goes.

If anybody else in your town can get rich, so can you; and if anybody else in your state can get rich, so can you.

Again, it is not a matter of choosing some particular business or profession. People get rich in every business, and in every profession; while their next-door neighbors in the same vocation remain in poverty.

It is true that you will do best in a business which you like, and which is congenial to you; and if you have certain talents which are developed, you will do best in a business which calls for the exercise of those talents.

Also, you will do best in a business which is suited to your locality; an ice-cream parlor would do better in a warm climate than in Greenland, and a salmon fishery will succeed better in the Northwest than in Florida, where there are no salmon.

But, aside from these general limitations, getting rich is not dependent upon your engaging in some particular business, but upon your learning to do things in a Certain Way. If you are now in business, and anybody else in your locality is getting rich in the same business, while you are not getting rich, it is because you are not doing the things in the same way that the other person is doing them.

No one is prevented from getting rich by lack of capital. True, as you get capital the increase becomes more easy and rapid; but one who has capital is already rich, and does not need to consider how to become so. No matter how poor you may be, if you begin to do things in the Certain Way you will begin to get rich; and you will begin to have capital. The getting of capital is a part of the process of getting rich; and it is a part of the result which invariably follows the doing of things in the Certain Way. You may be the poorest man on the continent, and be deeply in debt; you may have neither friends, influence, nor resources; but if you begin to do things in this way, you must infallibly begin to get rich, for like causes must produce like effects. If you have no capital, you can get capital; if you are in the wrong business, you can get into the right business; if you are in the wrong location, you can go to the right location; and you can do so *by beginning in your present business and in your present location* to do things in the Certain Way which causes success.

CHAPTER TWO ½

THE WORD "SCIENCE" CAN BE DEFINED BY the word system or principals. There is a concreteness of what science is. Getting rich does not happen with disorganization or by not following rules or principals. Doing specific things incorporates well within the system of science.

In order for you to carry out an experiment in science you need to think about what it is that you want to accomplish. What do you want to create in your mind? Do you want a great office with a fabulous desk? Do you want a large home with a pool? Do you want to create a business of service that everyone needs? Spend some time thinking about what it is that you want to create. Have fun with it!

Make sure that you are a little selfish and understand that the universe will take care of the rest. The idea that a reaction in chemistry will produce an end product should be a good rule of thumb for you and your mission to become rich. If the reaction of A + B = C is true, then we must think about what type of reaction is needed for us to become rich. A + B is the reaction. It produces C. C is our richness.

The idea of doing A + B, a certain way, will create a certain result, i.e. C. We can control our results by controlling our reaction. *The Science of Getting Rich* is the control of that reaction.

The idea is to do something a certain way to get a certain result. By doing something a certain way, you can guarantee the result every time. I find it fascinating that we try and make a living by working the reaction that other people have set up for us, rather than designing our own.

The idea that control is a major part of our arsenal as human beings is staggering. We can create and produce just about anything with the correct reaction. *The Science of Getting Rich* has to do with understanding what reaction is desired to produce the results that are needed. In other words, now that you have the notion that the universe will aid in creating anything, what is it that you want to produce? We will address that later in the book.

Do you feel the power or what?

CHAPTER THREE

♦IS OPPORTUNITY MONOPOLIZED?♦

NO MAN IS KEPT POOR BECAUSE opportunity has been taken away from him; because other people have monopolized the wealth, and have put a fence around it. You may be shut off from engaging in business in certain lines, but there are other channels open to you. Probably it would be hard for you to get control of any of the great railroad systems; that field is pretty well monopolized. But the electric railway business is still in its infancy, and others plenty of scope for enterprise; and it will be but a very few years until traffic and transportation through the air will become a great industry, and in all its branches will give employment to hundreds of thousands, and perhaps to millions, of people. Why not turn your attention to the development of aerial transportation, instead of competing with J.J. Hill and others for a chance in the steam railway world?

It is quite true that if you are a workman in the employ of the steel trust you have very little chance of becoming the owner of the plant in which you work; but it is also true that if you will commence to act in a Certain Way, you can soon leave the employ of the steel trust; you can buy a farm of from ten to forty acres, and engage in business as a producer of foodstuffs. There is great opportunity at this time for men who will live upon small tracts of land and cultivate the same intensively; such as men will certainly get rich. You may say that it is impossible for you to get the land, but I am going to prove to you that it is not impossible, and that you can certainly get a farm if you will go to work in a Certain Way.

At different periods the tide of opportunity sets in different directions, according to the needs of the whole, and the particular stage of social evolution which has been reached. At present, in America, it is setting toward agriculture and the allied industries and professions. Today, opportunity is open before the factory worker in his line. It is open before the business man who supplies the farmer more that before the one who supplies the factory worker; and before the professional man who waits upon the farmer more than before the one who serves the working class.

There is abundance of opportunity for the man who will go with the tide, instead of trying to swim against it.

So the factory workers, either as individuals or as a class, are not deprived opportunity. The workers are not being "kept down" by their masters; they are not being "grounded" by the trusts and combinations of capital. As a class, they are where they are because they do not do things in a Certain Way. If the workers of America chose to do so, they could follow the example of their brothers in Belgium and other countries, and establish great department stores and cooperative industries; they could elect men of their own class to office, and pass laws favoring the development of such cooperative industries; and in a few years they could take peaceable possession of the industrial field.

The working class may become the master class whenever they will begin to do things in a Certain Way; the law of wealth is the same for them as it is for all others. This they must learn; and they will remain where they are as long as they continue to do as they do. The individual worker, however, is not held down by the ignorance or the mental slothfulness of his class; he can follow the tide of opportunity to riches, and this book will tell him how.

No one is kept in poverty by a shortness in the supply of riches; there is more than enough for all. A palace as large as the capitol at Washington might be built for every family on earth from the building material in the United States alone; and under intensive cultivation, this country would produce wool, cotton, linen, and silk enough to cloth each person in the world finer than Solomon was arrayed in all his glory; together with food enough to feed them all luxuriously.

The visible supply is practically inexhaustible; and the invisible supply really is inexhaustible.

Everything you see on earth is made from one original substance, out of which all things proceed.

New Forms are constantly being made, and older ones are dissolving; but all are shapes assumed by One Thing.

There is no limit to the supply of Formless Stuff, or Original Substance. The universe is made out of it; but it was not all used in making the universe. The spaces in, through, and between the forms of the visible universe are permeated and filled with the Original Substance; with the formless Stuff; with the raw material of all things. Ten thousand times as much as has been made might still be made, and even then we should not have exhausted the supply of universal raw material.

No man, therefore, is poor because nature is poor, or because there is not enough to go around.

Nature is an inexhaustible storehouse of riches; the supply will never run short. Original Substance is alive with creative energy, and is constantly producing more forms. When the supply of building material is exhausted, more will be produced; when the soil is exhausted so that foodstuffs and materials for clothing will no longer grow upon it, is will be renewed or more soil will be made. When all the gold and silver has been dug from the earth, if man is still in such a stage of social development that he needs gold and silver, more will be produced from the Formless. The Formless Stuff responds to the needs of man; it will not let him be without any good thing.

This is true of man collectively; the race as a whole is always abundantly rich, and it individuals are poor, it is because they do not follow the Certain Way of doing things which makes the individual man rich.

The Formless Stuff is intelligent; it is stuff which thinks. It is alive, and is always impelled toward more life.

It is the natural and inherent impulse of life to seek to live more; it is the nature of intelligence to enlarge itself, and of consciousness to seek to extend its boundaries and find fuller expression. The universe of forms has been made by Formless Living Substance, throwing itself into form in order to express itself more fully.

The universe is a great Living Presence, always moving inherently toward more life and fuller functioning.

Nature is formed for the advancement of life; its impelling motive is the increase of life. For this cause, everything which can possibly minister to life is bountifully provided; there can be no lack unless God is to contradict Himself and nullify His own works.

You are not kept poor by lack in the supply of riches; it is fact which I shall demonstrate a little farther on that even the resources of the Formless Supply are at the command of the man or woman who will act and think in a Certain Way.

CHAPTER THREE ½

WALLACE WATTLES' QUESTION,

"is opportunity monopolized?" is one that makes for an interesting thought. What I have realized since I have ventured out into my entrepreneurial career is that life and business are founded on the principals of abundance, not scarcity. We are taught from a young age that life and business are built on the foundations of scarcity. Something that I think is a critical fundamental mistake when planning one's future.

Our future, for those that want it, is limitless with opportunities. If our creator had made our universe with a limited supply of resources, don't you think that would mean that our creator is limited? I don't subscribe to that notion. In business, resources are abundant, there for the taking, for those of you who want it. Is there a certain way that you need to go about it? Absolutely! You see that's part of your reaction…remember A + B? What is your C? Once you know what your C is, go out and get your reaction, your A and B.

Your A and B are abundant in the universe. They are everywhere. They are in a form called the "original substance", the substance that everything is made from. It is without form, but has mass. It is invisible, but can be seen in the human mind. It is an intelligent substance that can think. It is found in the very essence of who we are as a people. This substance has been talked about for a long time. The very aspect of who we are has conjured up notions of the substance. Remember, "I think, therefore I am". Renc Descartes famous statement tried to encompass this original substance.

Other well know speakers and thinkers of our day such as Wayne Dyer with his book *The Power of Intention,* also tried to shed some light on the original substance. He called it "the source" when he describes it in his talks and books. The source is the creator of everything. The source provides for the needs of life to advancement or development to a stronger level. Yet others try and control our thoughts both from a conscious and subconscious level to try and understand the original substance. Writers like Elkhart Tolle who has written books such as *The Power of Now* and *The New Earth* have explained this original substance that is often misused or not used at all by the human mind from a subconscious level. He discusses how the ego takes over instead of the source and how it works in a destructive way instead of a creative way.

If you start to think of things in more of an abundant way you will understand opportunity rather than fear. Scarcity is something that poses questions of fear in our minds. That fear is the mechanism that stops a reaction from happening or it might change the reaction so that your product is different than you had intended. Be careful of what your A and B are so that you can control your C.

Are you ready to go to the "lab of life" and take action yet?

CHAPTER FOUR

♦THE FIRST PRINCIPLE IN THE SCIENCE OF GETTING RICH♦

THOUGHT IS THE POWER WHICH CAN produce tangible riches from the Formless Substance. The stuff from which all things are made is a substance which thinks, and a thought of form in the substance produces the form.

Original Substance moves according to its thoughts; every form and process you see in nature is the visible expression of a thought in Original Substance. As the Formless Stuff thinks of a form, it takes that form; as it thinks of a motion, it makes that motion. That is the way all things were created. We live in a thought world, which is part of a thought universe. The thought of a moving universe extended throughout Formless Substance, and the Thinking Stuff moving according to that thought, took the form of systems of planets, and maintains that form. Thinking Substance takes the form of its thought, and moves according to the thought. Holding the idea of a circling system of suns and worlds, it takes the form of these bodies and moves them as it thinks. Thinking the form of these bodies, and moves them as it thinks. Thinking the form of a slow-growing oak tree, it moves according to the lines of motion it has established; the thought of an oak tree does not cause the instant formation of a full-grown tree, but it does start in motion the forces which will produce the tree, along established lines of growth.

Every thought of form, held in thinking Substance, causes the creation of the form, but always, or at least generally, along lines of growth and action already established.

The thought of a house of a certain construction, if it were impressed upon Formless Substance, might not cause the instant formation of the house; but it would cause the turning of creative energies already working in trade and commerce into such channels as to result in the speedy building of the house. And it there were no existing channels through which the creative energy could work, then the house would be formed directly from primal substance, without waiting for the slow processes of the organic and inorganic world.

No thought of form can be impresses upon Original Substance without causing the creation of the form.

Man is a thinking center, and can originate thought. All the forms that man fashions with his hands must first exist in his thought; he cannot shape a thing until he has thought that thing.

And so far man has confined his efforts wholly to the work of his hands; he has applied manual labor to the world of forms, seeking to change or modify those already existing. He has never thought of trying to cause the creation of new forms by impressing his thoughts upon Formless Substance.

When man has a thought-form, he takes material from the forms of nature, and makes an image of the form which is in his mind. He has, so far, made little or no effort to cooperative with Formless Intelligence; to work "with the Father." He has not dreamed that he can "do what he seeth the Father doing." Man reshapes and modifies existing forms by manual labor; he has given no attention to the question whether he may not produce things from Formless Substance by communicating his thoughts to it. We propose to prove that he may do so; to prove that any man or woman may do so, and to show how. As our first step, we must lay down three fundamental propositions.

First, we assert that there is one original formless stuff, or substance, from which all things are made. All the seemingly many elements are but different presentations of one element; all the many forms found in organic and inorganic nature are but different shapes, made from the same stuff. And this stuff is thinking stuff; a thought held in it produces shapes. Man is a thinking center, capable of original thought; if man can communicate his thought to original thinking substance, he can cause the creation, or formation, of the thing he thinks about. To summarize this:

There is a thinking stuff from which all things are made, and which, in its original state, permeates, penetrates, and fills the interspaces of the universe.

A thought, in this substance, produces the thing that is imaged by the thought.

Man can form things in his thought, and, by impressing his thought upon Formless Substance, can cause the thing he thinks about to be created.

It may be asked if I can prove these statements; and without going into details, I answer that I can do so, both by logic and experience.

Reasoning back from the phenomena of form and thought, I come to one original thinking substance; and reasoning forward from this thinking substance, I come to man's power to cause the formation of the thing he thinks about.

And by experiment, I find the reasoning true; and this is my strongest proof

If one man who reads this book gets rich by doing what it tells him to do, that is evidence in support of my claim; but if every man who does what it tells him to do gets rich, that is positive proof until someone goes through the process and fails. The theory is true until the process fails; and this process will not fail, for every man who does exactly what this book tells him to do will get rich.

I have said that men get rich by doing things in a Certain Way; and in order to do so, men must become able to think in a Certain Way.

A man's way of doing things is the direct result of the way he thinks about things.

To do things in a way you want to do them, you will have to acquire the ability to think the way you want to think; this is the first step toward getting rich,

To think what you want to think it to think TRUTH, *regardless of appearances.*

Every man has the natural and inherent power to think what he wants to think, but it requires far more effort to do so than it does to think the thoughts which are suggested by appearances. To think according to appearance is easy; to think truth regardless of appearance is laborious, and requires the expenditure of more power than any other work man is called upon to perform.

There is no labor from which most people shrink as they do from that of sustained and consecutive thought; it is the hardest work in the world. This is especially true when truth is contrary to appearances. Every appearance in the visible world tends to produce a corresponding form in the mind which observes it, and this can only be prevented by holding the thought of the TRUTH.

To look upon the appearance of disease will produce the form of disease in your own mind, and ultimately in your body, unless you hold the thought of the truth, which is that there is no disease; it is only an appearance, and the reality it health.

To look upon the appearance of poverty will produce corresponding forms in your own mind, unless you hold to the truth that there is no poverty; there is only abundance.

To think health when surrounded by the appearances of disease, or to think riches when in the midst of appearance of poverty, requires power; but he who acquires this power becomes a *master mind.* He can conquer fate; he can have what he wants.

This power can only be acquired by getting hold of the basic fact which is behind all appearances; and that fact is that there is one Thinking Substance, from which and by which all things are made.

Then we must grasp the truth that every thought held in this substance becomes a form, and that man can so impress his thoughts upon it as to cause them to take form and become visible things.

When we realize this, we lose all doubt and fear, for we know that we can create what we want to create; we can get what we want to have, and can become what we want to be. As a first step toward getting rich, you must believe the three fundamental statements given previously in this chapter; and in order to emphasize them, I repeat them here:

There is a thinking stuff from which all things are made, and which, in its original state, permeates, penetrates, and fills the interspaces of the universe.

A thought, in this substance, produces the thing that is imaged by the thought.

Man can form things in his thought, and, by impressing his thought upon Formless Substance, can cause the thing he thinks about to be created.

You must lay aside all other concepts of the universe that this monistic one; and you must dwell upon this until it is fixed in your mind, and has become your habitual though. Read these creed statements over and over again; fix every word upon your memory, and meditate upon them until you firmly believe what they say. If a doubt comes to you, cast it aside as a sin. Do not listen to arguments against this idea; do not go to churches or lectures where a contrary concept of things is taught or preached. Do not read magazines or books which teach a different idea; if you get mixed up in your faith, all your efforts will be in vain.

Do not ask why these things are true, nor speculate as to how they can be true; simply take them on trust.

The science of getting rich begins with the absolute acceptance of this faith.

CHAPTER FOUR ½

THIS CHAPTER PRESENTS THE READER with the start of the essence of the entire book. Where the rubber hits the road! Here, in this chapter, think of the original form as clay or play-doh (if you want to reminisce). The thoughts that you have as a person act as a mold. A mold used to make an image or to actually produce the beginnings of what it is you think about.

The original substance is there to be molded into your destiny, good or bad. You see, some people's destinies, good or bad, are done on purpose and other people's destinies are created on accident. What you think about you create. That's the specific reason that negative thinkers produce a negative life. Positive thinkers are usually in a position in life in which they are much more fulfilled.

The form that is created is caused by the thought in which gets impressed upon the original substance (clay). It is the power of the universe. It is our creator working in the most pure form. It is the reason that prayer works for so many people. It is the reason that meditation is so healthy. This form that is created by thought starts the reaction of you're A and B.

Think of that house that you want. Think of it in a way that presents a photograph or better yet a movie in your head. Involve all of your senses with the thought. What is looks like, what it smells like and how the front door feels when you open it. The more specific you are the better.

Sure enough once that starts to take place, the universe starts to take action. The universe prepares the commodities and labor involved to produce that house. It may not appear immediately, but by using continual thought to impress your vision upon the formless it becomes formed by the science that is involved.

I was impressed by this sentence: "I have said that men get rich by doing things in a certain way, and by doing so, men must become able to think in a certain way." I would like to modify Descartes well know statement to "I think, therefore I create". Creating through thought is empowering. I think it is something that makes the future bright. It makes the motivation of life become something that is permanent in our bloodstream, rather than just a quick high.

To think what you want to think is to think TRUTH, regardless of appearances. Thought of appearances are easy. You look at something and it causes thought. If you look at a poor person, you think poverty. If you look at sickness and disease you think of despair, unhappiness or even death. That doesn't take much effort, because that is how we are trained. I am not saying to not look at a poor person or someone riddled with disease. I am saying that when you look at those things, think about what you want to happen that is positive. Remember the form that gets created is what you are thinking about. Negative thoughts produce negative forms. I'm talking about creating your own image in your mind of how to change your world.

The power to think in a different way will cause you other benefits besides wealth. If done correctly and thoroughly it will cause you to live longer without sickness, enjoying all that life has to offer. It will also produce an environment that you can further develop life for both for you and those around you.

Can you believe the empowerment you are feeling?

CHAPTER FIVE

♦INCREASING LIFE♦

YOU MUST GET RID OF THE LAST VETIGE of the old idea that there is a Deity whose will it is that you should be poor, or who purposes may be served by keeping you in poverty.

The Intelligent Substance which is All, and in All, and which lives in All and lives in you, is a consciously Living Substance. Being a consciously living substance, it must have the nature and inherent desire of every living intelligence for increase of life. Every living thing must continually seek for the enlargement of its life, because life, in the mere act of living, must increase itself.

A seed, dropped into the ground, springs into activity, and in the act of living produces a hundred more seeds; life, by living, multiples itself. It is forever Becoming More; it must do so, if it continues to be at all.

Intelligence is under the same necessity for continuous increase. Every thought we think makes it necessary for us to think another thought; consciousness is continually expanding.

Every fact we learn leads us to the learning of another fact; knowledge is continually increasing. Every talent we cultivate brings to the mind the desire to cultivate another talent; we are subject to the urge of life, seeking expression, whichever drives us on to know more, to do more, and to be more.

In order to know more, do more, and be more we must have more; we must have things to use, for we learn, and do, and become, only by using things. We must get rich, so that we can live more.

The desire for riches is simply the capacity for larger life seeking fulfillment; every desire is the effort of an unexpressed possibility to come into action. It is power seeking to manifest which causes desire. That which makes you want more money is the same as that which makes the plant grow; it is Life, seeking fuller expression.

The One Living Substance must be subject to this inherent law of all life; it permeated with desire to live more; that is why it is under the necessity of creating things.

The One Substance desires to live more in you; hence it wants you to have all the things you can use.

It is the desire of God that you should get rich. He wants you to get rich because He can express Himself better through you if you have plenty of things to use in giving Him expression. He can live more in you if you have unlimited command of the means of life.

The universe desires you to have everything you want to have.

Nature is friendly to your plans.

Everything is naturally for you.

Make up your mind that this is true.

It is essential, however, that *your purpose should harmonize with the purpose that is in All.*

You must want real life, not mere pleasure of sensual gratification. Life is the performance of functions; and the individual really lives only when he performs every function, physical, mental, and spiritual, of which he is capable, without excess in any.

You do not want to get rich in order to live swinishly, for the gratification of animal desires; that is not life. But the performance of every physical function is a part of life, and no one lives completely who denies the impulses of the body a normal and healthful expression.

You do not want to get rich solely to enjoy mental pleasures, to get knowledge, to gratify ambition, to outshine others, to be famous. All these are a legitimate part of life, but the man who lives for the pleasures of intellect alone will only have a partial life, and he will never be satisfied with his lot.

You do not want to get rich solely for the good of others, to lose yourself for the salvation of mankind, to experience the joys of philanthropy and sacrifice. The joys of the souls are only a part of life; and they are no better or nobler than any other part.

You want to get rich in order that you may eat, drink, and be merry when it is time to do these things; in order that you may surround yourself with beautiful things, see distant lands, feed your mind, and develop your intellect; in order that you may love men and do kind things, and be able to play a good part in helping the world to find truth.

But remember that extreme altruism is no better and no nobler than extreme selfishness; both are mistakes.

Get rid of the idea that God wants you to sacrifice yourself for others, and that you can secure His favor by doing so; God requires nothing of the kind.

What He wants is that you should make the most of yourself, for yourself, and for others; and *you can help others more by making the most of yourself than in any other way.*

You can make the most of yourself only by getting rich; so it is right and praiseworthy that you should give your first and best thought to the work of acquiring wealth.

Remember, however, that the desire of Substance is for all, and its movements must be for more life to all; it cannot be made to work for less life to any, because it is equally in all, seeking riches and life.

Intelligent Substance will make things for you, but it will not take things away from someone else and give them to you.

You must get rid of the thought of competition. You are to create, not to compete for what is already created.

You do not have to take anything away from anyone.

You do not have to drive sharp bargains.

You do not have to cheat, or to take advantage. You do not need to let any man work for you for less than he earns.

You do not have to covert the property of others, or to look at it with wishful eyes. No man has anything of which you cannot have the like, and that without taking what he has away from him.

You are to become a creator, not a competitor; you are going to get what you want, but in such a way that when you get it every other man will have more than he has now.

I am aware that there are men who get a vast amount of money by proceeding in direct opposition to the statements in the paragraphs above, and may add a word of explanation here. Men of the plutocratic type, who become very rich, do so sometimes purely by their extraordinary ability on the plane of competition; and sometimes they unconsciously relate themselves to

Substance in its great purposes and movements for the general racial upbuilding through industrial evolution. Rockefeller, Carnegie, Morgan, et al., have been the unconscious agents of the Supreme in the necessary work of systematizing and organizing productive industry; and in the end, their work will contribute immensely toward increased life for all. Their day is nearly over; they have organized production, and *will soon be succeeded by the agents of the multitude, who will organize the machinery of distribution.*

The multi-millionaires are like the monster reptiles of the prehistoric eras; they play a necessary part in the evolutionary process, but the same Power which produced them will dispose of them. And it is well to bear in mind that they have never been really rich; a record of the private lives of most of this class will show that they have really been the most abject and wretched of the poor.

Riches secured on the competitive plane are never satisfactory and permanent; they are yours today, and another's tomorrow. Remember, if you are to become rich in a scientific and Certain Way, you must rise entirely out of the competitive thought. You must never think for a moment that the supply is limited. Just as soon as you begin to think that all the money is being "cornered" and controlled by bankers and others, and that you must exert yourself to get laws passed to stop this process, and so on—in that moment you drop into the competitive mind, and your power to cause creation is gone for the time being; and what is worse, you will probably arrest the creative movements you have already instituted.

Know that there are countless millions of dollars' worth of gold in the mountains of the earth, not yet brought to light; and know that if there were not, more would be created from Thinking Substance to supply your needs.

Know that the money you need will come, even if it is necessary for a thousand men to be led to the discovery of new gold mines tomorrow.

Never look at the visible supply; look always at the limitless riches in Formless Substance, and know that they are coming to you as fast as you can receive and use them. Nobody, by concerning the visible supply, can prevent you from getting what is yours.

So never allow yourself to think for an instant that all the best building sports will be taken before you get ready to build your house, unless you hurry. Never worry about the trust and combines, and get anxious for fear they will soon come to own the whole earth. Never get afraid that you will lose what you want because some other person "beats you to it." That cannot possibly happen; you are causing what you want to be created from Formless Substance, and the supply is without limits. Stick to the formulated statement:

There is a thinking stuff from which all things are made, and which, in its original state, permeates, penetrates, and fills the interspaces of the universe.

A thought, in this substance, produces the thing that is imaged by the thought.

Man can form things in his thought, and, by impressing his thought upon Formless Substance, can cause the thing he thinks about to be created.

CHAPTER FIVE ½

THERE ARE SO MANY CHAPTERS OF THIS book that I could name my favorite. This one is definitely one of those chapters. This chapter is titled "Increasing life", which is the mere sole of biology. I like the fact that this book as a whole and particularly this chapter speaks of abundance.

Everything from creation of the universe, to the biology and chemistry that it took for us to even be here on this planet, is nothing short of amazing. Can you imagine the odds or chances that were present for us to be here in the first place? Our creator must have strength and intelligence that is unfathomable to our human minds. I appreciate this book so much because of the positive message throughout.

I think it is also a little controversial, which I like. It talks about the fact that God desires us to be rich. I have to think back in my understandings and studies of the great religions of the world. I think that there is a common thread that entwines all. That thread is the idea of humbleness of who we are. I think that in our own human minds, man has taken that and ran with the thought that to be humble, you do not have to be rich.

Let me say that I am not trying to make you think or feel a certain way about religion. I want you to know that I have not been the biggest fan of religion because of how it seems to be organized. It brings more of mankind into the equation rather than the divinity of God. I would much rather get involved in spiritualism than religion. It is in spiritualism that I think richness comes into play. We have a great responsibility to enrich our lives so that we can fully be engulfed in our spiritualism.

When we are engulfed in our spiritualism, we have the time to explore all of the great religions of the world. We can also go further with that exploration to identify the different denominations and sects of the religion we follow. The idea of exploring within our own mind what we look to as our creator is exciting and mind blowing. The other thing that I do not necessarily like about religion is the competition that is present in the world today.

Interesting enough, we explore the idea of competition in this chapter also. I like the fact that Wallace Wattles explains that competition should not be involved in getting rich. In the universe, abundance is the theme rather than scarcity. Scarcity produces competition. Consider your own path. Create the best. It's not a competitive thing. Think of it as a betterment of life and I think you will find opportunity abound and limitless wealth throughout the universe.

Will you be able to lose the idea of being a competitor and becoming a creator? Does this image ring a bell with the divinity of God?

CHAPTER SIX

♦HOW RICHES COME TO YOU♦

WHEN I SAY THAT YOU DO NOT HAVE to drive sharp bargains, I do not mean that you do not have to drive any bargains at all, or that you are above the necessity for having any dealings with your fellow men. I mean that you will not need to deal with them unfairly; you do not have to get something for nothing, but can give to every man more than you take from him.

You cannot give every man more in cash market value than you take from him, but you can give him more in use values than the cash values of the thing you take from him. The paper, ink, and other material in this book may not be worth the money you pay for it; but if the ideas suggested by it bring you thousands of dollars, you have not been wronged by those who sold it to you; they have given you are great use value for a small cash value.

Let us suppose that I own a picture by one of the greatest artists, which, in any civilized community, is worth thousands of dollars. I take it to Baffin Ray, and by "salesmanship" induce an Eskimo to give a bundle of furs worth $500 for it. I have really wronged him, for he has no use for the picture; it has no use value to him; it will not add to his life.

But suppose I give him a gun worth $50 for his furs; then he has made a good bargain. He has use for the gun; it will get him many more furs and much more food; it will add to his life in every way; it will make him rich.

When you rise from the competitive to the creative plane, you can scan your business transactions very strictly, and if you are selling any man anything which does not add more to his life than the thing he gives you in exchange, you can afford to stop it. You do not have to beat anybody in business. And if you are in a business which does beat people, get out of it at once.

Give every man more in use value than you take from him in cash value; then you are adding to the life of the world by every business transaction.

If you have people working for you, you must take from them more in cash value than you pay them in wages; but you can so organize your business that it will be filled with the principle of advancement, and so that each employee who wishes to do so may advance a little every day.

You can make your business do for your employees that this book is doing for you. You can so conduct your business that it will be a sort of ladder, by which every employee who will take the trouble may climb to riches himself; and given the opportunity, if he will not do so it is not your fault.

And finally, because you are to cause the creation of your riches from Formless Substance which permeates all your environment, it does not follow that they are to take shape from the atmosphere and come into being before your eye.

If you want a sewing machine, for instance, I do not mean to tell you that you are to impress the thought of a sewing machine on Thinking Substance until the machine is formed without hands, in the room where you sit, or elsewhere. But if you want a sewing machine, hold the mental image of it with the most positive certainty that it is being made, or is on its way to you. After once forming the thought, have the most absolute and unquestioning faith that the sewing machine is coming; never think of it, or speak of it, in any other way than as being sure to arrive. Claim it as already yours.

It will be brought to you by the power of the Supreme Intelligence, acting upon the minds of men. If you live in Maine, it may be that a man will be brought from Texas or Japan to engage in some transaction which will result in the getting what you want.

If so, the whole matter will be as much to that man's advantage as it is to yours.

Do not forget for a moment that the Thinking Substance is through all, in all, communicating with all, and can influence all. The desire of Thinking Substance for fuller life and better living has caused the creation of all the sewing machines already made; and it can cause the creation of millions more, and will, whenever men set it in motion by desire and faith, and by acting in a Certain Way.

You can certainly have a sewing machine in your house; and it is just as certain that you can have any other thing or things which you want, and which you will use for the advancement of your own life and the lives of others.

You need not hesitate about asking largely; "it is your Father's pleasure to give you the kingdom," said Jesus.

Original Substance wants to live all that is possible in you, and wants you to have all that you can or will use for the living of the most abundant life.

If you fix upon your consciousness the fact that the desire you feel for the possession of riches is one with the desire of Omnipotence for more complete expression, your faith becomes invincible.

Once I saw a little boy sitting at a piano, and vainly trying to bring harmony out of the keys; and I saw that he was grieved and provoked by his inability to play real music. I asked him the cause of his vexation, and he answered, "I can feel the music in me, but I can't make my hands go right." The music in him was the *urge* of Original Substance, containing all the possibilities of all life; all that there is of music was seeking expression through the child.

God, the One Substance, is trying to live and do and enjoy things through humanity. He is saying "I want hands to build wonderful structures, to play diving harmonies, to paint glorious pictures; I want feet to run My errands, eyes to see My beauties, tongues to tell mighty truths and to sing marvelous songs," and so on.

All that there is of possibility is seeking expression through men. God wants those who can play music to have pianos and every other instrument, and to have the means to cultivate their talents to the fullest extent; He wants those who can appreciate beauty to be able to surround themselves with beautiful things; He wants those who can discern truth to have every opportunity to travel and observe; He wants those who can appreciate dress to be beautifully clothed, and those who can appreciate good food to be luxuriously fed.

He wants all these things because it is Himself that enjoys and appreciates them; it is God who wants to play, and sing, and enjoy beauty, and proclaim truth and wear fine clothes, and eat good foods. "It is God that worketh in you to will and to do," said Paul.

The desire you feel for riches is the infinite, seeking to express Himself in you as He sought to find Himself in you as He sought to find expression in the little boy at the piano.

So you need not hesitate to ask largely.

Your part is to focalize and express the desire to God.

This is a difficult point with most people; they retain something of the old idea that poverty and self-sacrifice are pleasing to God. They look upon poverty as a part of the plan, a necessity of nature. They have the idea that God has finished His work, and made all that He can make, and that the majority of men must stay poor because there is not enough to go around. They hold to so much of this erroneous thought that they feel ashamed to ask for wealth; they try not to want more than a very modest competence, just enough to make them fairly comfortable.

I recall now the case of one student who was told that he must get in mind a clear picture of the things he desired, so that the creative thought of them might be impressed on Formless Substance. He was a very poor man, living in a rented house, and having only what he earned from day to day; and he could not grasp the fact that all wealth was his. So, after thinking the matter over, he decided that he might reasonably ask for a new rug for the floor of his best room, and an anthracite coal stove to heat the house during the cold weather. Following the instructions given in this book, he obtained these things in a few months; and then it dawned upon him that he had not asked enough. He went through the house in which he lived, and planned all the improvements he would like to make in it; he mentally added a bay window here and a room there, until it was complete in his mind as his ideal home; and then he planned its furnishings.

Holding the whole picture in his mind, he began living in the Certain Way, and moving toward what he wanted; and he owns the house now, and is rebuilding it after the form of his mental image. And now, with still larger faith, he is going on to get greater things. It has been unto him according to his faith, and it is so with you and with all of us.

CHAPTER SIX ½

IN THIS CHAPTER WE START TO THINK

and discuss how the riches begin to come to you. This chapter is a classic business model. When we talk about value in business we must consider what is being exchanged. It usually is money, goods or service. Here we understand that it is not the money, goods or service that is important, but the perception or perceived value.

Give every man more in use value than you take from him in cash value. Then you are adding to the life of the world by every business transaction. If someone can take a product or service and purchase it from you and then take it to make a better life or increase his or her life, then that is what is most important. It actually should be the target of every marketing and sales force in the world!

I also like the idea of acting as if. When you act as if, you can change the gearing in your mind. When you do that you change your physical world. When you do not know how to do something, act as if you do and take some kind of action. Let the universe guide you. When you are thinking of what you want with wealth and with other things, act as if you already have them.

I can tell you I came from very meager means growing up, but I always thought that I had it better than everyone else. I had always appreciated everything that I got and knew that it was the best for me at the time. In my first book, *Real Estate H20*, I gave the story of me growing up in a single parent home. I always thought of things that I wanted and really made myself feel as if I already had them. I tried to put my mind in the situation. Even before I read *The Science of Getting Rich*, it seems that has always been my mode of operation. I always dreamed and pretended. My dreams always seemed to become my reality. Wallace Wattles just verified what I've always known.

Subconsciously, when you dream, the feelings are the same whether they become reality or not. Let me repeat that in a different way. Your subconscious mind cannot tell the difference between realty and make believe. *The Science of Getting Rich* is the idea that what you create in you mind comes true because the universe does everything in its power to give you that. The formless substance imprints the form and creates what we think about.

Hello…are you feeling as powerful as I am?

CHAPTER SEVEN

♦GRATITUDE♦

THE ILLUSTRATIONS GIVING IN THE LAST chapter will have conveyed to the reader the fact that the first step toward getting rich is to convey the idea of your wants to the Formless Substance.

This is true, and you will see that in order to do so it becomes necessary to relate yourself to the Formless Intelligence in a harmonious way.

To secure this harmonious relation is a matter of such primary and vital importance that I shall give some space to its discussion here, and five you instructions which, if you will follow them, will be certain to bring you into perfect unity of mind with God.

The whole process of mental adjustment and atonement can be summed up in one word, gratitude.

First, you believe that there is on Intelligent Substance, from which all things proceed; second, you believe that this Substance gives you everything you desire; and third, you relate yourself to it by a feeling of deep and profound gratitude.

Many people who order their lives rightly in all other ways are kept in poverty by their lack of gratitude. Having received on gift from God, they cut the wired which connect them with Him by failing to make acknowledgment.

It is easy to understand that the nearer we live to the source of wealth, the more wealth we shall receive; and it is easy also to understand that the soul that is always grateful lives in closer touch with God than the one which never looks to Him in thankful acknowledgment.

The more gratefully we fix our minds on the Supreme when good things come to us, the more good things we will receive, and the more rapidly they will come; and the reason simply is that the mental attitude of gratitude draws the mind into closer touch with the source from which the blessings come.

If it is a new thought to you that gratitude brings your whole mind into closer harmony with the creative energies of the universe, consider it well, and you will see that it is true. The good things you already have have come to you along the line of obedience to certain laws. Gratitude will lead your mind out along the ways by which things come; and it will keep you in close harmony with creative thought and prevent you from falling into competitive thought.

Gratitude alone can keep you looking toward the All, and prevent you from falling into the error of thinking of the supply as limited; and to do that would be fatal to your hopes.

There is a Law of Gratitude, and it is absolutely necessary that you should observe the law, if you are to get the results you seek.

The Law of Gratitude is the natural principle that action and reaction are always equal, and in opposite directions.

The grateful outreaching of your mind in thankful praise to the Supreme is a liberation or expenditure of force; it cannot fail to reach that to which it addressed, and the reaction is an instantaneous movement towards you.

"Draw nigh unto God, and He will draw nigh unto you." That is a statement of psychological truth.

And if your gratitude is strong and constant, the reaction in Formless Substance will be strong and continuous; the movement of the things you want will be always toward you. Notice the grateful attitude that Jesus took; how He always seems to be saying, "I thank Thee Father, that Thou hearest me," You cannot exercise much power without gratitude; for it is gratitude that keeps you connected with Power.

But the value of gratitude does not consist solely in getting you more blessings in the future. Without gratitude you cannot long keep from dissatisfied thought regarding things as they are.

The moment you permit your mind to dwell with dissatisfaction upon things as they are, you begin to lose ground. You fix attention upon the common, the ordinary, the poor, and the squalid, and the mean; and your mind takes the form of these things. Then you will transmit these forms or mental images to the Formless, and the common, the poor, the squalid, and the mean will come to you.

To permit your mind to dwell upon the inferior is to become inferior and to surround yourself with inferior things.

On the other hand, to fix your attention on the best is to surround yourself with the best, and to become the best.

The Creative Power within us makes us into the image of that to which we give our attention.

We are Thinking Substance, and thinking substance always takes the form of that which it thinks about.

The grateful mind is constantly fixed upon the best; therefore it tends to become the best; it takes the form or character of the best, and will receive the best.

Also, faith is born of gratitude. The grateful mind continually expects good things, and expectation becomes faith. The reaction of gratitude upon one's own mind produces faith; and every outgoing wave of grateful thanksgiving increases faith. He who has no feeling of gratitude cannot long retain a living faith; and without a living faith you cannot get rich by the creative method, as we shall see in the following chapters.

It is necessary, then, to cultivate that habit of being grateful for every good thing that comes to you; and to give thanks continually.

And because all things have contributed to your advancement, you should include all things in your gratitude.

Do not waste time thinking or talking about the shortcomings or wrong actions of plutocrats of trust magnates. Their organization of the world has made your opportunity; all you get really comes to you because of them.

Do not rage against corrupt politicians; if it were not for politicians we should fall into anarchy, and your opportunity would be greatly lessened.

God has worked a long time and very patiently to bring us up to where we are in industry and government, and He is going right on with His work. There is not the least doubt that He will do away with plutocrats, trust magnates, captains of industry, and politicians as soon as they can be spared; but in the meantime, behold they are all very good. Remember that they are all helping to arrange the lines of transmission along which your riches will come to you, and be grateful to them all. This will bring you into harmonious relations with the good in everything, and the good in everything will move toward you.

CHAPTER 7 ½

THE EARTH IS ESTIMATED TO BE 4.5 billion years old. Modern man has been on the earth for an estimated 25,000 years. Can you imagine the time before man? It was an eternity. What had to happen for man to appear and evolve to where we are today? There were so many critical factors. Everything had to be just right.

What about the creation of our planet, our solar system, our galaxy and our universe? How precise did things have to happen to get up to the point of where we are today? I am amazed and can get lost in thinking about the precision of our creator. The intellectual thought of this idea can keep me busy for hours. I am also overwhelmed by the feeling of gratitude.

Something I have to continually improve is my practice of gratitude. It is apparent that it is such an important aspect of human life, yet it is often the last thing that we do or think about. Think about it, we say thank you after we have been given something. I have been truly blessed in my life. I had a ball in getting to this point. I have the best children and I am excited for what the future has in store. I have always tried to take an inventory of things that I need to work on in my life. Believe me, sometime the list is longer than I want. Practicing gratitude is definitely one of them.

No matter how bad a situation gets, we should always put ourselves in a position of gratitude. We need to be thankful for what we have, so that the creator can provide more in our future. Without gratitude, there is no room for abundance. Without gratitude, there is no security.

In giving gratitude to the source of everything, what most people refer to as God, it really makes you feel that you sometimes throw that out to the universe with no one really hearing you. If you use the statement that is consistently repeated throughout the book, it will tell you that the source, our God, the formless intelligence is everywhere.

There is a thinking stuff from which all things are made, and which, in its original state, permeates, penetrates, and fills the interspaces of the universe.

A thought, in this substance, produces the thing that is imagined by the thought.

Man can form things in his thought, and, by impressing his thought upon formless substance, can cause the thing he thinks about to be created.

Did I say thank you?

CHAPTER EIGHT

♦THINKING IN A CERTAIN WAY♦

TURN BACK TO CHAPTER 6 AND READ again the story of the man who formed a mental image of his house, and you will get a fair idea of the initial step toward getting rich. You must for a clear and definite mental picture of what you want; you cannot transmit an idea unless you have it yourself.

You must have it before you can give it; and many people fail to impress Thinking Substance because they have themselves only a vague and misty concept of the things they want to do, to have, or to become.

It is not enough that you should have a general desire for wealth "to do good with "; everybody has that desire.

It is not enough that you should have a wish to travel, see things, live more, etc. Everybody has those desires also. If you were going to send a wireless message to a friend, you would not send the letters of the alphabet in their order, and let him construct the message for himself; nor would you take words at random from the dictionary. You would send a coherent sentence; one which meant something. When you try to impress your wants upon Substance, remember that it must be done by a coherent statement; you must know what you want, and be definite. You can never get rich, or start the creative power, by sending out unformed longings and vague desires.

Go over you desires just as the man I have described went over his house; see just what you want, and get a clear mental picture of it as you wish it to look when you get it.

That clear mental picture you must have continually in mind, as the sailor has in mind the port toward which he is sailing the ship; you must keep your face toward it all the time. You must no more lose sight of it that the steersman loses sight of the compass.

It is not necessary to take exercises in concentration, nor to set apart special times for prayer and affirmation, nor to "go into the silence,: nor to do occult stunts of any kind. These things are well enough, but all you need is to know what you want, and to want it badly enough so that it will stay in your thoughts.

Spend as much of your leisure time as you can in contemplating your picture, but no one needs to take exercises to concentrate his mind on a thing which he really wants; it is the things you do not really care about which require effort to fix your attention upon them.

And unless you really want to get rich, so that the desire is strong enough to hold your thoughts directed to the purpose as the magnetic pole holds the needle of the compass, it will hardly be worthwhile for you to try to carry out the instructions given in this book.

The methods herein set forth are for people whose desire for riches is strong enough to overcome mental laziness and the love of ease, and make them work.

The more clear and definite you make your picture then, and the more you dwell upon it, bringing out all its delightful details, the stronger your desire will be; and the stronger your desire, the easier it will be to hold your mind fixed upon the picture of what you want.

Something more is necessary, however, than merely to see the picture clearly. If that is all you do, you are only a dreamer, and will have little or no power for accomplishment.

Behind your clear vision must be the purpose to realize it; to bring it out in tangible expression.

And behind this purpose must be an invincible and unwavering FAITH that the thing is already yours; that it is "at hand" and you have only to take possession of it.

Live in the new house, mentally, until it takes form around you physically. In the mental realm, enter at once into full enjoyment of the things you want.

"Whatsoever things ye ask for when ye pray, believe that ye receive them, and ye shall have them," said Jesus.

See the things you want as if they were actually around you all the time; see yourself as owning and using them. Make use of them in imagination just as you will use them when they are your tangible possessions. Dwell upon your mental picture until it is clear and distinct, and then take the Mental Attitude of Ownership toward everything in that picture. Take possession of it, in mind, in the full faith that it is actually yours. Hold to this mental ownership; do not waiver for an instant in the faith that it is real.

And remember what was said in a proceeding chapter about gratitude; be as thankful for it all the time as you expect to be when it has taken form. The man who can sincerely thank God for the things which as yet he owns only in imagination, has real faith. He will get rich; he will cause the creation of whatsoever he wants.

You do not need to pray repeatedly for things you want; it is not necessary to tell God about it every day.

"Use not vain repetitions as the heathen do," said Jesus said to His pupils, "for your Father knoweth that ye have need of these things before ye ask Him."

Your part is to intelligently formulate your desire for the things which make for a larger life, and to get these desires arranged into a coherent whole; and then to impress this Whole Desire upon the Formless Substance, which has the power and the will to bring you what you want.

You do not make this impression by repeating strings of words; you make it by holding the vision with unshakable

PURPOSE to attain it, and with steadfast FAITH that you do attain it.

The answer to prayer is not according to your faith while you are talking, but according to your faith while you are working.

You cannot impress the mind of God by having a special Sabbath day set apart to tell Him what you want, and the forgetting Him during the rest of the week. You cannot impress Him by having special hours to go into your closet and pray, if you then dismiss the matter from your mind until the hour of prayer comes again.

Oral prayer is well enough, and has its effect, especially upon yourself, in clarifying your vision and strengthening your faith; but it is not your oral petitions which get you what you want. In order to get rich you do not need a "sweet hour of prayer"; you need to "pray without ceasing." And by prayer I mean holding steadily to your vision, with the purpose to cause its creation into solid form, and the faith that you are doing so.

"Believe that ye receive them."

The whole matter turns on receiving, once you have clearly formed your vision. When you have formed it, it is well to make an oral statement, addressing the Supreme in reverent prayer; and from that moment you must, in mind, receive what you ask for. Live in the new house; wear the fine clothes; ride in the automobile; go on the journey, and confidently plan for greater journeys. Think and speak of all the things you have asked for in terms of actual present ownership. Imagine an environment, and a financial condition exactly as you want them, and live all the time in that imaginary environment and financial condition. Mind, however, that you do not do this as a mere dreamer and castle builder; hold to the FAITH that the imaginary is being realized, and to the PURPOSE to realize it. Remember that it is faith and purpose in the use of the imagination which make the difference between the scientist and the dreamer. And having learned this fat, it is here that you must learn the proper use of the Will.

CHAPTER EIGHT ½

WHEN I WAS IN SCHOOL, I REMEMBER doing reports throughout the years. For instance, when I was in the fifth grade, our teacher asked us to do a report on a topic of our choice. I remember picking the Earth as my topic. I distinctively remember that she told me that it was too vague. "If you are going to do a report on the earth, you could possibly be writing for years", she said.

As I got older and was in high school, I actually enjoyed writing and wanted to further my skills. I remember taking a rhetoric class which focused on writing structure. I remember my teacher explaining the idea of something called a picture-frame paragraph. A picture–frame paragraph is a paragraph that actually gives your mind a very vivid vision of what is being read.

I remember that lesson. I want you to know that the more detailed that you can be with your thoughts, the better. I have actually practiced this technique quite often and I can tell you that I am amazed every time I come across physically what was thought of or created in my mind.

This vivid imagination thing has always been a double edged sword for me. For instance, with my imagination, I always had the propensity to "disturb others" during class. In third grade it had gotten so bad that my teacher, Mrs. Poole, actually told me she hated me! Can you believe that? As she said this in front of the rest of the class, I saw my classmates with their mouths wide open. It was at that moment I realized I was special! My imagination continued. In fifth grade, Mrs. Vliek thought it was best for my desk and I to be put into a cardboard refrigerator box for a semester so that I would not "disturb others". Did she really think that six feet high cardboard walls could contain me? I took lemons and made lemonade. I figured that I was the first kid in America with his own cubicle!

I do an exercise at some of my workshops that help people in moving toward their goals. I want people to focus on their reason why, rather than focusing on their goals. I have people decide what their reason why is; the reason why they are doing something in the first place. There is always an underlying reason someone does something. For example, people want money, perhaps so they do not have to work. Their actual reason is to spend more time with family. That is their WHY. In other words, WHY are they interested in real estate investing or correcting their credit? In most cases, it's not the idea of real estate investing or correcting their credit that drives them; it's something more than that. It usually is what the investment in real estate gives them or what having good credit will enable them to do. Usually it's more time with their family or being able to do the things that they love.

These are things that should drive them rather than their goals, such as buying a 20-unit apartment building. When you can get that specific and have your reason WHY drive you instead of goals, you will have fuel that is much more meaningful and longer lasting. It's not that I do not want you to have goals, I do. I would like you to use a different fuel that most people. I would like you to surround yourself with the ideas in Wallace Wattles book that will deliver everything you need and want. Use your goals as your road and your reason "why" as the fuel in the car to get you down the road.

It's the specificity that I need you to have when deciding what you want. Keep that mental picture of wealth or richness. If it is a house that you desire, make sure you know that house like the palm of your hand. Understand, as we have mentioned previously, all of the five senses that you have must go into imaging what the house looks like, feels like, smells like, sounds like and tastes like. Tastes like? Yes, what does the water taste like out of the tap! That's how detailed I would like you to get!

Interestingly enough, that's the first step. The next step, is to actually imagine that you live in that house. You have to at this point believe that you actually have what you are dreaming of. I know this sounds a little absurd at this point. I would have thought it would have too until I read *The Science of Getting Rich.*

It has explained to me in blueprint form just how I have been able to accomplish what I do. I just didn't know it until I completed the book. That is also why I have felt compelled to give you my thoughts in my own book, *The Alchemy of Wealth.*

Finally, I think you should carry this thought process with you all of the time. You have to make sure that this is a staple in your routine. Create in your mind what you want. Act as if you already have it, and implement that in your daily activity. If you do this, your results will be controlled by your actions, which will be controlled by your thoughts. The question is, "do you have the will?"

CHAPTER NINE

♦HOW TO USE THE WILL♦

TO SET ABOUT GETTING RICH IN A scientific way, you do not try to apply your will power to anything outside of yourself.

Your have to right to do so, anyway.

It is wrong to apply your will to other men and women, in order to get them to do what you wish done.

It is as flagrantly wrong to coerce people by mental power as it is to coerce them by physical power. If compelling people by physical force to do things for you reduces them to slavery, compelling them by mental means accomplishes exactly the same thing; the only difference is in methods. If taking things from people by physical force is robbery, them taking things by mental force is robbery also; there is no difference in principal.

You have no right to use your will power upon another person, even "for his own good"; for you do not know what is for his good. The science of getting rich does not require you to apply power or force to any other person, in any way whatsoever. There is not the slightest necessity for doing so; indeed, any attempt to use your will upon others will only tend to defeat your purpose.

You do not need to apply your will to things, in order to compel them to come to you.

That would simply be trying to coerce God, and would be foolish and useless, as well as irreverent.

You do not have to compel God to give you good things, anymore than you have to use your will power to make the sun rise.

You do not have to use your will power to conquer an unfriendly deity, or to make stubborn and rebellious forces do your bidding.

Substance is friendly to you, and is more anxious to give you what you want than you are to get it.

To get rich, you need only to use your will power upon yourself.

When you know what to think and do, then you must use your will to compel yourself to think and do the right things. That is the legitimate use of the will in getting what you want--to use it in holding yourself to the right course. Use your will to keep yourself thinking and acting in the Certain Way.

Do not try to project your will, or your thoughts, or your mind out into space, to "act" on things or people.

Keep your mind at home; it can accomplish more there than elsewhere.

Use your mind to form a mental image of what you want, and to hold that vision with faith and purpose, and use your will to keep your mind working in the Right Way.

The more steady and continuous your faith and purpose, the more rapidly you will get rich, because you will make only *positive* impressions upon Substance; and you will not neutralize or offset them by negative impressions.

The picture of your desires, held with faith and purpose, is taken up by the Formless, and permeates it to great distances--throughout the universe, for all I know.

As this impression spreads, all things are set moving toward its realization; every living thing, every inanimate thing, and the things yet uncreated, are stirred toward bringing into being that which you want. All force begins to be exerted in that direction, all things begin to move toward you. The minds of people, everywhere, are influenced toward doing the things necessary to the fulfilling of your desires, and they work for you, unconsciously.

But you can check all this by starting a negative impression in the Formless Substance. Doubt or unbelief is as certain to start a movement away from you as faith and purpose are to start one toward you. It is by not understanding this that most people who try to make use of "mental science" in getting rich make their failure. Every hour and moment you spend in giving heed to doubts and fears, every hour you spend in worry, every hour in which your soul is possessed by unbelief, sets a current away from you in the whole domain of Intelligent Substance. All the promises are unto them that believe and unto them only. Notice how insistent Jesus was upon this point of belief; and now you know the reason why.

Since belief is all important, it behooves you to guard your thoughts; and as your beliefs will be shaped to a very great extent by the things you observe and think about, it is important that you should command your attention.

And here the will comes into use; for it is by your will that you determine upon what things your attention shall be fixed.

If you want to become rich, you must not make a study of poverty.

Things are not brought into being by thinking about their opposites. health is never to be attained by studying disease and thinking about disease; righteousness is not to be promoted by studying sin and thinking about sin; and no one ever got rich by studying poverty and thinking about poverty.

Medicine as a science of disease has increased disease; religion as a science of sin has promoted sin, and economics as a study of poverty will fill the world with wretchedness and want.

Do not talk about poverty; do not investigate it, or concern yourself with it. Never mind what its causes are; you have nothing to do with them.

What concerns you is the cure.

Do not spend your time in charitable work, or charity movements; all charity only tends to perpetuate the wretchedness it aims to eradicate.

I do not say that you should be hard hearted or unkind, and refuse to hear the cry of need; but you must not try to eradicate poverty in any of the conventional ways. Put poverty behind you, and put all that pertains to it behind you, and "make good."

Get rich, that is the best way you can help the poor.

And you cannot hold the mental image which is to make you rich if you fill your mind with pictures of poverty. Do not read books or papers which give circumstantial accounts of the wretchedness of the tenement dwellers, of the horrors of child labor, and so on. Do not read anything which fills your mind with gloomy images of want and suffering.

You cannot help the poor in the least by knowing about these things; and the widespread knowledge of them does not tend at all to do away with poverty.

What tends to do away with poverty is not getting pictures of poverty into your mind, but getting pictures of wealth into the minds of the poor.

You are not deserting the poor in their misery when you refuse to allow your mind to be filled with pictures of that misery.

Poverty can be done away with, not by increasing the number of well-to-do people who think about poverty, but by increasing the number of poor people who purpose with faith to get rich.

The poor do not need charity; they need inspiration. Charity only sends them a loaf of bread to keep them alive in their wretchedness, or gives them an entertainment to make them forget for an hour or two; but inspiration will cause them to rise out of their misery. If you want to help the poor, demonstrate to them that they can become rich; prove it by getting rich yourself.

The only way in which poverty will ever be banished from this world is by getting a large and constantly increasing number of people to practice the teachings of this book.

People must be taught to become rich by creation, not by competition.

Ever man who becomes rich by competition throws down behind him the ladder by which he rises, and keeps others down; but every man who gets rich by creation opens a way for thousands to follow him, and inspires them to do so.

You are not showing hardness of heart or an unfeeling disposition when you refuse to pity poverty, see poverty, read about poverty, or think or talk about it, or listen to those who do talk about it. Use your will power to keep your mind *off* the subject of poverty, and to keep it fixed with faith and purpose *on* the vision of what you want.

CHAPTER NINE ½

THIS CHAPTER HAS MADE AS MUCH OF AN impact on me as any chapter in the book. I think this chapter has prompted me to keep the book with me at all times. When I first started to read the book I was instantly brought back to the movie *Star Wars* where one of the heroes of the movie, Luke Skywalker, is faced with the idea of using his power for evil instead of good.

This chapter has also showed me how powerful our mind really is. I believe we can do anything that we set our minds to. I also like the idea of keeping our will to do positive things. To do positive things and to have what we want and need means that we must stay clear of negative thoughts.

To think in a negative manor is to negate our fruits. To think in a negative manor is to negate our closeness to our source or creator. To think in a negative way also brings us to a point where we are stagnant instead of changing. Changing is a way that we perpetually move forward. Remember our goal is to advance or develop life.

The most important thing that made such an impact from me from this chapter is when it discussed handling poverty. It talks about the idea of not concerning ourselves with poverty. At first, I must say, this disturbed me. I am involved heavily with a lot of charities and I wondered if this was going to destroy the whole book for me. I was wrong, it has increased my resolve that this may be one of the books that has not only shaped my life, but it may be the most important guideline for creating my future!

I am honored to sit on the Board of Directors for The Caring House Foundation. Its founder and good friend, Frank McKinney (Frank-McKinney.com) understands poverty. The foundation's mission is to build sustainable villages in third world countries. Frank always says that we are not in the charity business, but the sustainability and empowerment business.

I traveled to Haiti several times in 2008 to witness that very idea. Because the unemployment rate in Haiti is over 90% (yes, I said 90%) we use all local labor. We make our villages self-sustaining by introducing tilapia ponds, animal husbandry and onsite wells for clean water. I challenge you to get involved with the ideas of sustainability and empowerment for some of the world's most challenging issues. If you would like to sponsor a home or part of a village that we are currently building contact me through my website. I guarantee it will be life changing!

In this chapter Wallace Wattles says, "Do not talk about poverty; do not investigate it; or concern yourself with it. Never mind what the causes are; you have nothing to do with them."

(This is the point where I felt a little uncomfortable, and then I read the next sentence).

"What concerns you is the cure."

Wow! How many times have you heard of national charities that have seemed to have been around for a long time and have not put a dent in the problem at hand! That means to me that they have been focusing on the symptoms instead of finding a cure for the problem. That might be easier said than done. But then I read this next sentence and I think it instantly changed how I approach things like poverty.

"What tends to do away with poverty is not getting pictures of poverty into your mind, but getting pictures of wealth into he minds of the poor."

As I read that statement I couldn't help but think about how powerful this material that you're reading in this book is. It can not only change what we do as individuals, but I think we can change mankind. Will we change what we know and who we are or stay as we are? Are we really developing life in a positive way if we don't take action on this information?

CHAPTER TEN

♦FURTHER USE OF THE WILL♦

YOU CANNOT RETAIN A TRUE AND CLEAR vision of wealth if you are constantly turning your attention to opposing pictures, whether they be external or imaginary.

Do not tell of your past troubles of a financial nature, if you have had them, do not think of them at all. Do no tell of the poverty of your parents, or the hardships of your early life; to do any of these things is to mentally class yourself with the poor for the time being, and it will certainly check the movement of things in your direction.

"Let the dead bury their dead," as Jesus said.

Put poverty and all things that pertain to poverty completely behind you.

You have accepted a certain theory of the universe as being correct, and are resting all your hopes of happiness on its being correct; and what can you gain by fibbing heed to conflicting theories?

Do not read religious books which tell you that the world is soon coming to an end; and do not read the writing of muckrakers and pessimistic philosophers who tell you that it is going to the devil.

The world is not going to the devil; it is going to God.

It is wonderful Becoming.

True there may be a good many things in existing conditions which are disagreeable; but what is the use of studying them when they are certainly passing away, and when the study of them only tends to check their passing and keep them with us? Why give time and attention to things which are being removed by evolutionary growth, when you can hasten their removal only by promoting the evolutionary growth as far as your part of it goes?

No matter how horrible in seeming may be the conditions in certain countries, sections, or places, you waste your time and destroy your own chances by considering them.

You should interest yourself in the world's becoming rich.

Think of the riches the world is coming into, instead of the poverty it is growing out of; and bear in mind that the only way in which you can assist the world in growing rich is by growing rich yourself through the creative method--not the competitive one.

Give your attention wholly to riches; ignore poverty.

Whenever you think or speak of those who are poor, think and speak of them as those who are becoming rich; as those who are to be congratulated rather than pitied. Then they and others will catch the inspiration, and begin to search for the way out.

Because I say that you are to give your whole time and mind and thought to riches, it does not follow that you are to be sordid or mean.

To become really rich is the noblest aim you can have in life, for it includes everything else.

On the competitive plane, the struggle to get rich is a Godless scramble for power over other men; but when we come into the creative mind, all this is changed.

All that is possible in the way of greatness and soul unfoldment, of service and lofty endeavor, comes by way of getting rich; all is made possible by the use of things.

If you lack for physical health, you will find that the attainment of it is conditional on your getting rich.

Only those who are emancipated from financial worry, and who have the means to live a carefree existence and follow hygienic practices, can have and retain health.

Moral and spiritual greatness is possible only to those who are above the competitive battle for existence; and only those who are becoming rich on the plane of creative thought are free from the degrading influences of competition. If your heart is set on domestic happiness, remember that love flourishes best where there is refinement, a high level of through, and freedom from corrupting influences; and these are to be found only where riches are attained by the exercise of creative thought, without strife or rivalry.

You can aim at nothing so great or noble, I repeat, as to become rich; and you must fix your attention upon your mental picture of riches, to the exclusion of all that may tend to dim or obscure the vision.

You must learn to see the underlying TRUTH in all things; you must see beneath all seemingly wrong conditions the Great One Life ever moving forward toward fuller expression and more complete happiness.

It is the truth that there is no such thing as poverty; that there is only wealth.

Some people remain in poverty because they are ignorant of the fact that there is wealth for them; and these can best be taught by showing them the way to affluence in your own person and practice.

Others are poor because, while they feel that there is a way out, they are too intellectually indolent to put forth the mental effort necessary to find that way and travel it; and for these the very best thing you can do is to arouse their desire by showing them the happiness that comes from being rightly rich.

Others still are poor because, while they have some notion of science, they have become so swamped and lost in the maze of metaphysical and occult theories that they do not know which road to take. They try a mixture of many systems and fail in all. For these, again, the very best thing to do is to show the right way in your own person and practice, an ounce of doing things is worth a pound of theorizing.

The very best thing you can do for the whole world is to make the most of yourself.

You can serve God and man in no more effective way than by getting rich; that is, if you get rich by the creative method and not by the competitive one.

Another thing. We assert that this book gives in detail the principles of the science of getting rich; and if that is true, you do not need to read any other book upon the subject. This may sound narrow and egotistical, but consider; there is no more scientific method of computation in mathematics than by addition, subtraction, multiplication, and division; no other method is possible. There can be but one shortest distance between two points. There is only one way to think scientifically, and that is to think in the way that leads by the most direct and simple route to the goal. No man has yet formulated a briefer or less complete "system" than the one set forth herein' it has bee stripped of all non-essentials. When you commence on this, lay all others aside, put them out of your mind all together.

Read this book everyday; keep it with you; commit it to memory, and do not think about other "systems" and theories. If you do, you will begin to have doubts, and to be uncertain and wavering in your thought; and then you will begin to make failures.

After you have made good and become rich, you may study other systems as much as you please; but until you are quite sure that you have gained what you want, do not read anything on this line but this book, unless it be the authors mentioned in the preface.

And read only the most optimistic comments on the world's news; those in harmony with your picture.

Also, postpone your investigations into the occult. Do not dabble in theosophy, Spiritualism, or kindred studies. It is very likely that the dead still live, and are near; but if they are, let them alone; mind your own business.

Wherever the spirits of the dead may be, they have their own work to do, and their own problems to solve; and we have no right to interfere with them. We cannot help them, and it is very doubtful whether they can help us, or whether we have any right to trespass upon their time if they can. Let the dead and the hereafter alone, and solve your won problems; get rich. If you begin to mix with the occult, you will start mental cross-currents which will surely bring your hopes to shipwreck. Now, this and the preceding chapters have brought us to the following statement of basic facts--

There is a thinking stuff from which all things are made, and which, in its original state, permeates, penetrates, and fills the interspaces of the universe.

A thought, in this substance, produces the thing that is imaged by the thought.

Man can form things in his thought, and, by impressing his thought upon Formless Substance, can cause the thing he thinks about to be created.

In order to do this, man must pass from the competitive to the creative mind, he must form a clear mental picture of the things he wants, and hold this picture in his thoughts with the fixed PURPOSE *to get what he wants, and the unwavering* FAITH *that he does get what he wants, closing his mind against all that may tend to shake his purpose, dim his vision, or quench his faith.*

And in addition to all this, we shall now see that he must live and act in a Certain Way.

CHAPTER TEN ½

I AM OFTEN INTERESTED IN ANY information that can guide people into the arena where they can have success. I understand more and more why Wallace Wattles is making a distinction between the creative side and the competitive side. There is a time and place for competition and wealth creation may not be one of them. I think that may be surprising for a lot of people.

I also like the idea of not concerning oneself of past financial troubles. Your financial past does not define who you are. So many times I see people that are negative about life and it is mostly because of what they experienced in their past. So every single day is a fresh start with regard to understanding wealth and how to achieve it. I would use this idea to focus on the future of yourself and what action you need to take.

Make the distinction of the idea of past financial misfortunes. Learn from the mistake, as not to reproduce it in the future, not carry it with you as a burden that will cause negative thoughts or inhibits action.

As I am writing this portion of the book we have just experienced one the great downturns in our economic history (March 2009). The sediment around the U.S. and the world seems to be that the world is going to end. I'm sure by the time you are reading this book you will have a whole new outlook as to the world events and economy. Surely, the world is not ending anytime soon.

Do not get yourself caught up in the negativity that seems to be that of an epidemic. Business, real estate and our economy will always run in cycles. When you discover this you should always know that you can profit greatly from downturns in the economy. Please refer to chapter 10 in my book *Real Estate H20* for more information about business and real estate cycles. Two other books I recommend you read about this subject are *Burst This!*, written by Frank McKinney and *The Next Great Bubble Boom*, written by Harry Dent.

As I have made it a habit to eliminate any negative news items from my daily activity (CNN, FOX, CNBC, etc.) I think that Wallace Wattles was on to something when he wrote this chapter. Negativity spurs negativity, just as success spurs success. T.V. has a way of putting someone else's mind pictures in your head (I don't want anyone else in there)!

I have realized something else by reading this chapter. I realized that people probably throughout time have thought that the world was going to end and that negativity is preached as a way to make some people feel better or to sensationalize life. Wealth sensationalizes life, nothing else.

The other thing that I love about this chapter is the idea that people get so involved in the metaphysical and occult theories. They get paralyzed in taking any action because they become confused in which road to take. I compare that to the education seminar business. Throughout my seminars, I meet people that have spent a ton of money on their education, but have not taken any action.

My advice to them is to stay focused on one thing instead of trying to master all. Wealth creation is hard work. There is no magic pill or "easy button" from *Staples*. Keep yourself into the mode of taking action. When you continuously take action you will be able to look back after a series of small steps only to realize you have covered great ground. Refer to my website for free conference calls that I do to keep you on track.

What are you going to do?

CHAPTER ELEVEN

♦ACTING IN THE CERTAIN WAY♦

THOUGHT IS THE CREATIVE POWER, OR the impelling force which causes the creative power to act; thinking in a Certain Way will bring riches to you, but you must not rely upon thought alone, paying no attention to personal action. That is the rock upon which many otherwise scientific metaphysical thinkers meet shipwreck--the failure to connect thought with personal action.

We have not yet reached the stage of development, even supposing such a stage to be possible, in which man can create directly from Formless Substance without nature's processes or the work of human hands; man must not only think, but his personal action must supplement his thought.

By thought you can cause the gold in the hearts of the mountains to be impelled toward you; but it will not mine itself, refine itself, coin itself into double eagles, and come rolling along the roads seeking its way into your pocket.

Under the impelling power of the Supreme Spirit, men's affairs will be so ordered that someone will be led to mine the gold for you, other men's business transactions will be so directed that the gold will be brought toward you, and you must so arrange your own business affairs that you may be able to receive it when it comes to you.

Your thought makes all things, animate and inanimate, work to bring you what you want; but your personal activity must be such that you can rightly receive what you want when it reaches you. You are not to take it as charity, nor to steal it; you must give every man more in use value than he gives you in cash value.

The scientific use of thought consists in forming a clear and distinct mental image of what you want; in holding fast to the purpose to get what you want; and in realizing with grateful faith that you do get what you want.

Do not try to "project" your thought in any mysterious or occult way, with the idea of having it go out and do things for you; that is wasted effort, and will weaken your power to think with sanity.

The action of thought in getting rich is fully explained in the preceding chapters; your faith and purpose positively impress your vision upon Formless Substance, which has *the same desire for more life that you have,* and this vision, received from you, sets all the creative forces at work *in and through their regular channels of action*, but directed toward you.

It is not your part to guide or supervise the creative process; all you have to do with that is to retain your vision, stick to your purpose, and maintain your faith and gratitude.

But you must act in a Certain Way, so that you can appropriate what is yours when it comes to you; so that you can meet the things you have in your picture, and put them in their proper places as they arrive.

You can really see the truth of this. When things reach you, they will be in the hands of other men, who will ask an equivalent for them.

And you can only get what is yours by giving the other man what is his.

Your pocketbook is not going to be transformed into a Fortunata's purse, which shall be always full of money without effort on your part.

This is the crucial point in the science of getting rich; right here where thought and personal action must be combined. There are very many people who, consciously or unconsciously, set the creative forces in action by the strength and persistence of their desires, but who remain poor because they do not provide for the reception of the thing they want when it comes.

By thought, the thing you want is brought to you; by action you receive it.

Whatever your action is to be, it is evident that you must act *now*. You cannot act in the past, and it is essential to the clearness of your mental vision that you dismiss the past from your mind. You cannot act in the future, for the future is not here yet. And you cannot tell how you will want to act in any future contingency until that contingency has arrived.

Because you are not in the right business, or the right environment now, do not think that you must postpone action until you get into the right business or environment. And do not spend time in the present taking thought as to the best course in possible future emergencies; have faith in your ability to meet any emergency when it arrives.

If you act in the present with your mind on the future, your present action will be with a divided mind, and will not be effective.

Put your whole mind into present action.

Do not give your creative impulse to Original Substance, and then sit down and wait for results; if you do, you will never get them. Act now. There is never any time but now, and there never will be any time but now. If you are ever to begin to make ready for the reception of what you want, you must begin now.

And your action, whatever it is, must most likely be in your present business or employment, and must be upon the persons and things in your present environment.

You cannot act where you are not; you cannot act where you have been, and you cannot act where you are going to be; you can act only where you are.

Do not bother as to whether yesterday's work was well done or ill done; do today's work well.

Do not try to do tomorrow's work now; there will be plenty of time to do that when you get to it.

Do not try, by occult or mystical means, to act on people or things that are out of your reach.

Do not wait for a change of environment, before you act; get a change of environment by action.

You can so act upon the environment in which you are now, as to cause yourself to be transferred to a better environment.

Hold with faith and purpose the vision of yourself in the better environment, but act upon your present environment with all your heart, and with all your strength, and with all your mind.

Do not spend any time in daydreaming or castle building, hold to the one vision of what you want, and act *now*.

Do not cast about seeking some new thing to do, or some strange, unusual, or remarkable action to perform as a first step toward getting rich. It is probable that your actions, at least for some time to come, will be those you have been performing for sometime past; but you are to begin now to perform these actions in the Certain Way which will surely make you rich.

Do not feel discouraged, or sit down and lament because you are misplaced. No man was ever so misplaced but that he could not find the right place, and no man ever became so involved in the wrong business but that he could not get into the right business.

Hold the vision of yourself in the right business, with the purpose to get into it, and the faith that you will get into it, and are getting into it; but *act* in your present business. Use your present business as the means of getting a better one, and use your present environment as the means of getting into a better one. Your vision of the right business, if held with faith and purpose, will cause the Supreme to move the right business toward you; and your action, if performed in the Certain Way, will cause you to move toward the business.

If you are an employee, or wage earner, and feel that you must change places in order to get what you want, do not "project" your thought into space and rely upon it to get you to another job. It will probably fail to do so.

Hold the vision of yourself in the job you want, while you *act* with faith and purpose on the job you have, and you will certainly get the job you want.

Your vision and faith will set the creative force in motion to bring it toward you, and your action will cause the forces in your own environment to move you toward the place you want. In closing this chapter, we will add another statement to our syllabus--

There is a thinking stuff from which all things are made, and which, in its original state, permeates, penetrates, and fills the interspaces of the universe.

A thought, in this substance, produces the thing that is imaged by the thought.

Man can form things in his thought and by impressing his thought upon Formless Substance, can cause the thing he thinks about to be created.

In order to do this, man must pass from the competitive to the creative mind, he must form a clear mental picture of the things he wants, and hold this picture in his thoughts with the fixed PURPOSE *to get what he wants, and the unwavering* FAITH *that he does get what he wants, closing his mind to all that may tend to shake his purpose, dim his vision, or quench his faith.*

That he may receive what he wants when it comes, man must act now *upon the people and things in his present environment.*

CHAPTER ELEVEN ½

AS I HAVE SAID WITH CHAPTERS before…this may be my favorite chapter. I guess that's why I am writing a grown up version of a book report on *The Science of Getting Rich*! This chapter acts as a parent scolding a child. We have for too long in America wanted to find wealth by taking the easy route. Unfortunately, anyone who has obtained wealth easily usually loses it just as easy.

Wealth is something that you create in your mind and imprint on the formless substance and then the connection between your mind and the rest of the universe starts to take over. That mechanism, that action, is a two way street. Surely the universe will do everything it can to create what you have imagined. Why? Well, it improves life. It secures life. And it perpetuates life. The reason that we are here at all.

The other side of the street is the one where you claim responsibility by taking action. If you want to gain wealth through real estate, for instance, you have to submerge yourself in that life. Join a real estate investment club, talk with real estate professionals and start putting out offers. If it is the car business that you would like to obtain wealth in you have to join car clubs, maybe go to an automotive plant, or maybe even spend some time in Detroit, the Mecca for the car industry.

With that in mind…take some time and create what you want. This is a great chance to think about what you enjoy. I truly believe that you will enjoy the journey much more if you involve yourself in something that excites you. Ask someone how their life is when they don't enjoy their job. They will tell you their life sucks. Our careers play such an important role in our overall happiness.

I think it also plays so much into our stress level. Stress is nothing more than a feeling of being out of control. Not controlling what you do on a daily basis is primarily responsible for creating an underlying stress that people handle in different ways. Some good, some bad. You know me, I can't give you a problem without providing a solution. If you are feeling stress in your life it's probably because your not doing what Wallace Wattles says in this chapter of the book. ***Take Action!!! Massive Action!!*** You will get the control back by doing that consistently.

By taking action with regard to all aspects of your life you really obtain both control and a feeling of progress. Human beings need both of those in their life. That is probably what drives the laws that govern success that Wallace Wattles talks about. If that's the case, then wealth and the obtainment of wealth goes so much deeper than just monetary value. Wealth should be defined as everything but monetary. It's what money can buy you that is the object of desire. Please read the last two sentences again. (Okay, one time is enough! This isn't wash, rinse, repeat on your shampoo bottle!)

As you remember from my first book, *Real Estate H2O*, I talked about my five freedoms in life: Financial, Time, Relationship, Spiritual and Physical. What are your freedoms? Are you moving toward them or away from them? Have you used the power of the universe to create what you want? Are you taking action to get you there? Are you waiting for tomorrow? If you are waiting for tomorrow, then you have to go back through this chapter and notice that you can only control one time aspect. The present. You cannot control the past, you cannot control the future. Stop adding stress, stop making excuses and live in the NOW!

Do you have self awareness of the present?

CHAPTER TWELVE

♦EFFICIENT ACTION♦

YOU MUST USE YOUR THOUGHT AS directed in previous chapters, and begin to do what you can do where you are; and you must do *all* that you can do where you are.

You can advance only by being larger than your present place; and no man is larger than his present place who leaves undone any of the work pertaining to that place.

The world is advanced only by those who more than fill their present places.

If no man quite filled his present place, you can see that there must be a going backward in everything. Those who do not quite fill their present places are dead weight upon society, government, commerce, and industry; they must be carried along by others at a great expense. The progress of the world is retarded only by those who do not fill the places they are holding; they belong to a former age and a lower stage or plane of life, and their tendency is toward degeneration. No society could advance if every man was smaller than his place; social evolution is guided by the law of physical and mental evolution. In the animal world, evolution is caused by excess of life.

When an organism has more life than can be expressed in the functions of its own plane, it develops the organs of a higher plane, and a new species is originated.

There never would have been new species had there not been organisms which more than filled their places. The law is exactly the same for you; your getting rich depends upon your applying this principle to your own affairs.

Everyday is either a successful day or a day of failure; and it is the successful days which get you what you want. If every day is a failure, you can never get rich; while if everyday is a success, you cannot fail to get rich.

If there is something that may be done today, and you do not do it, you have failed insofar as that thing is concerned; and the consequences may be more disastrous than you imagine.

You cannot foresee the results of even the most trivial act; you do not know the workings of all the forces that have been set moving in your behalf. Much may be depending on your doing some simple act; it may be the very thing which is to open the door of opportunity to very great possibilities. You can never know all the combinations which Supreme Intelligence is making for you in the world of things and of human affairs; your neglect or failure to do some small thing may cause a long delay in getting what you want.

Do, every day, *all* that can be done that day.

There is, however, a limitation or qualification of the above that you must take into account.

You are not to overwork, nor to rush blindly into your business in the effort to do the greatest possible number of things in the shortest possible time.

You are not to try to do tomorrow's work today, nor to do a week's work in a day.

It is really not the number of things you do, but the efficiency *of each separate action that counts.*

Every act is, in itself, either a success or a failure.

Every act is, in itself, either effective or inefficient.

Every inefficient act is a failure, and if you spend your life in doing inefficient acts, your whole life will be a failure.

The more things you do, the worse for you, if all your acts are inefficient ones.

On the other hand, every efficient act is a success in itself, and if every act of your life is an efficient one, your whole life *must* be a success.

The cause of failure is doing too many things in an inefficient manner, and not doing enough things in an efficient manner.

You will see that it is a self-evident proposition that if you do not do any inefficient acts, and if you do a sufficient number of efficient acts, you will become rich. If, now, it is possible for you to make each act an efficient one, you see again that the getting of riches is reduced to an exact science, like mathematics.

The matter turns, then, on the questions whether you can make each separate act a success in itself. And this you can certainly do.

You can make each act a success, because *all* Power is working with you; and *all* Power cannot fail.

Power is at your service; and to make each act efficient you have only to put power into it.

Every action is either strong or weak; and when everyone is strong, you are acting in the Certain Way which will make you rich.

Every act can be made strong and efficient by holding your vision while you are doing it, and putting the whole power of you FAITH and PURPOSE into it.

It is at this point that the people fail who separate mental power from personal action. They use the power of mind in one place and at one time, and they act in another place and at another time. So their acts are not successful in themselves; too many of them are inefficient. But if *all* Power goes into every act, no matter how commonplace, every act will be a success in itself, and as in the nature of things every success opens the way to other successes, your progress toward what you want, and the progress of what you want toward you, will become increasingly rapid.

Remember that successful action is cumulative in its results. Since the desire for more life is inherent in all things, when a man begins to more toward larger life more things attach themselves to him, and the influence of his desire is multiplied.

Do, every day, all that you can do that day, and do each act in an efficient manner.

I'm saying that you must hold your vision while you are doing each act, however trivial or commonplace, I do not mean to say that it is necessary at all times to see the vision distinctly to its smallest details. It should be the work of your leisure hours to use your imagination on the details of your vision, and to contemplate them until they are firmly fixed upon memory. If you wish speedy results, spend practically all your spare time in this practice.

By continuous contemplation you will get the picture of what you want, even to the smallest details, so firmly fixed upon your mind, and so completely transferred to the mind of Formless Substance, that in your working hours you need only to mentally refer
to the picture to stimulate your faith and purpose, and cause your best effort to be put forth. Contemplate your picture in your leisure hours until your consciousness is so full of it that you can grasp it instantly. You will become so enthused with its

bright promises that the mere thought of it will call forth the strongest energies of your whole being.

Let us again repeat our syllabus, and by slightly changing the closing statements bring it to the point we have now reached.

There is a thinking stuff from which all things are made, and which, in its original state, permeates, penetrates, and fills the interspaces of the universe.

A thought, in this substance, produces the thing that is imaged by the thought.

Man can form things in his thought, and, by impressing his thought upon Formless Substance, can cause the thing he thinks about to be created.

In order to do this, man must pass from the competitive to the creative mind, he must form a clear mental picture of the things he wants, and do, with faith and purpose, all that can be done each day, doing each separate thing in an efficient manner.

CHAPTER TWELVE ½

I THINK THIS STATEMENT FROM THE chapter says it all: "The World is Only Advanced by Those Who More Than Fill Their Present Places". I can remember being on vacation several times in my life and have felt the need to jump right back to my work. I think I have found a place in my life where I really enjoy what I do on a daily basis. So much so that I rather leave vacation to get back to work!

Have you ever met or knew someone that you thought could do more with their life? Have you ever met someone that you thought is doing more in life than humanly possible? This chapter is addressing those two things. No one can expect to accomplish things by not being as much as he or she could be.

I believe a person must stretch themselves to the point where they don't think they can make it. I can remember countless hours of playing basketball in elementary school and then into my high school years. I remember the drills that made me think that I was really pushing my body physically and wondered if I would make it. It is amazing, but those very drills, where I wondered if I would be able to make it physically, were the very thing that enabled me to play basketball at the collegiate level!

I believe the same to be true in entrepreneurism. I believe the same in wealth creation. Focusing on things that may seem to put you into an unfamiliar situation may make you think that you may not be able to handle it, such as facing the fears of your credit report. That very exercise of facing your fear of finding out what is on your credit report and your credit score and wondering whether you can handle it, may be the thing that propels you to the next level in wealth.

You have to be more than who you are! You have to make you current situation such that you overcome obstacles. I have always prided myself in making the best out of my situation so that I could be on a better playing ground with my creativity. Even when I know my situation in life wasn't as good as others, I created my own environment that was the best quality. (Remember the refrigerator box?)

I had a professor in college that always used to instill in us that whatever the situation that we were in, as far as our careers, it was the best at that particular moment. If it wasn't, it meant that we had no control. By giving up control you lose the ability to create, participate and prove yourself. Those are the very things that enable you to advance in your career and life.

This is what drives me to wonder about the time that everyone spends. Remember, everyone starts out with the same amount of time (24 hours a day) in their time bank account (as long as we are alive). Do you have a budget for spending that time? Are you spending time with people or on things that will not give you a return? Ah ha! Did that make you think? Now take action with the answers to those questions!

Are you going to take action?

CHAPTER THIRTEEN

♦GETTING INTO THE RIGHT BUSINESS♦

SUCCESS, IN ANY PARTICULAR BUSINESS, depends for one thing upon your possessing in a well-developed state the faculties required in that business.

Without good musical faculty no one can succeed as a teacher of music; without well-developed mechanical faculties no one can achieve great success in any of the mechanical trades; without tact and the commercial faculties no one can succeed in mercantile pursuits. But to possess in a well-developed state the faculties required in your particular vocation does not insure getting rich. There are musicians who have remarkable talent, and who yet remain poor; there are blacksmiths, carpenters, and so on who have excellent mechanical ability, but who do not get rich; and there are merchants with good faculties for dealing with men who nevertheless fail.

The different faculties are tools; it is essential to have good tools, but it is also essential that the tools should be used in the Right Way. One man can take a sharp saw, a square, a good plane, and so on, and build a handsome article of furniture; another man can take the same tools and set to work to duplicate the article, but his production will be a botch. He does not know how to use good tools in a successful way.

The various faculties of your mind are the tools with which you must do the work which is to make you rich; it will be easier for you to succeed if you get into a business for which you are well equipped with mental tools.

Generally speaking, you will do best in that business which will use your strongest faculties; the one for which you are naturally "best fitted." But there are limitations to this statement, also. No man should regard his vocation as being irrevocably fixed by the tendencies with which he was born.

You can get rich in *any* business, for if you have not the right talents for it, you can develop that talent; it merely means that you will have to make your tools as you go along, instead of confining yourself to the use of those with which you were born. It will be *easier* for you to succeed in a vocation for which you already have the talents in a well-developed state, but you *can* succeed in any vocation, for you can develop any rudimentary talent, and there is no talent of which you have not at least the rudiment.

You will get rich most easily in point of effort, if you do that for which you are best fitted; but you will get rich most satisfactorily if you do that which you *want* to do.

Doing what you want to do is life; and there is no real satisfaction in living if we are compelled to be forever doing something which we do not like to do, and can never do what we want to do. And it is certain that you can do what you want to do, the *desire* to do it is proof that you have within you the power which *can* do it.

Desire is a manifestation of power.

The desire to play music is the power which can play music seeking expression and development; the desire to invent mechanical devices is the mechanical talent seeking expression and development.

Where there is no power, either developed or underdeveloped, to do a thing, there is never any desire to do that thing; and where there is strong desire to do a thing, it is certain proof that the power to do it is strong, and only requires to be developed and applied in the Right Way.

All things else being equal, it is best to select the business for which you have the best developed talent; but if you have a strong desire to engage in any particular line of work, you should select that work as the ultimate end at which you aim.

You can do what you want to do, and it is your right and privilege to follow the business or avocation which will be most congenial and pleasant.

You are not obliged to do what you do not like to do, and should not do it except as a means to bring you to the doing of the thing you want to do.

If there are past mistakes whose consequences have placed you in an undesirable business or environment, you may be obliged for some time to do what you do not like to do; but you can make the doing of it pleasant by knowing that it is making it possible for you to come to the doing of what you want to do.

If you feel that you are not in the right vocation, do not act too hastily in trying to get into another one. The best way, generally, to change business or environment is by growth.

Do not be afraid to make a sudden and radical change if the opportunity is presented, and you feel after careful consideration that it is the right opportunity; but never take sudden or radical action when you are in doubt as to the wisdom of doing so.

There is never any hurry on the creative plane; and there is no lack of opportunity.

When you get out of the competitive mind you will understand that you never need to act hastily. No one else is going to beat you to the thing you want to do; there is enough for all. If one space is taken, another and a better one will be opened for you a little farther on; there is plenty of time. When you are in doubt, wait. Fall back on the contemplation of your vision, and increase your faith and purpose; and by all means, in times of doubt and indecision, cultivate gratitude.

A day or two spent in contemplating the vision of what you want, and in earnest thanksgiving that you are getting it, will bring your mind into such close relationship with the Supreme that you will make no mistake when you do act.

There is a mind which knows all there is to know; and you can come into close unity with this mind by faith and the purpose to advance in life, if you have deep gratitude.

Mistakes come from acting hastily, or from acting in fear or doubt, or in forgetfulness of the Right Motive, which is more life to all, and less to none.

As you go on in the Certain Way, opportunities will come to you in increasing number; and you will need to be very steady in your faith and purpose, and to keep in close touch with the All Mind by reverent gratitude.

Do all that you can do in a perfect manner every day, but do it without haste, worry, or fear. Go as fast as you can, but never hurry.

Remember that in the moment you begin to hurry you cease to be a creator and become a competitor; you drop back upon the old plane again.

Whenever you find yourself hurrying, call a halt; fix your attention on the mental image of the thing you want, and begin to give thanks that you are getting it. The exercise of *gratitude* will never fail to strengthen your faith and renew your purpose.

CHAPTER THIRTEEN ½

WHAT TO DO WITH WHAT YOU HAVE.

What or where is the direction that you are going to head to acquire wealth? What tools do you have? What tools do you need?

With the right tools I think it is possible for you to do anything with the right amount of action. Our first stop towards wealth has to be a self inventory of what tools are in our arsenal. Once you find that, then and only then, you can start to make progress in achieving wealth.

You may find that you have tools that you have never used before. You may find that you are missing tools that you will definitely need. You may also find that based on your inventory, you may change your path to wealth. It amazes me because most people never get to this place in their personal development. They constantly wonder why they have not accomplished more. They often wonder, "what if I would have"? If you do that, you are not doing what is says in the book, by living in the present. You are living in the past. Then you have the opposite of that by saying "someday…". By doing that you are living in the future. Either way they are loser mentalities.

I would really take some time and make a list of the things that you like to do. Create a list of things that you are passionate about. You will have a better chance at success if you do something that you love to do. I love real estate. I love to talk and teach about real estate. I love walking through old buildings. I love apartment buildings. That is my passion. Most of my business' are fashioned in some way around real estate. I have found easier success there because I have a lot of the tools necessary to succeed. The tools I did not have, I either went out and got or I made them myself.

You might think about that last statement and think…"made them himself"? When I first was getting into real estate, I made sure that I became a sponge in regards to learning. By learning about apartment buildings, financing and property management I could utilize those tools with my real estate investing. Real estate investing for me was the right business.

The right business for you may be all kinds of things like marketing, insurance or entertainment. By taking an inventory of yourself and the tools that you have you will find what will be the right business for you. Let your passions guide you. You then become what you love, you will love yourself more for that and people will love you more because of that.

Are you in love with something you could turn into a career?

CHAPTER FOURTEEN

♦THE IMPRESSION OF INCREASE♦

WHETHER YOU CHANGE YOUR VOCATION or not, your actions FOR the present must be those pertaining to the business in which you are now engaged.

You can get into the business you want by making constructive use of the business you are already established in; by doing your daily work in a Certain Way.

And insofar as your business consists in dealing with other men, whether personally or by letter, the key-thought of all your efforts must be to convey to their minds the impression of increase.

Increase is what all men and all women are seeking; it is the urge of the Formless Intelligence within them, seeking fuller expression.

The desire for increase is inherent in all nature; it is the fundamental impulse of the universe. All human activities are based on the desire for increase; people are seeking more food, more clothes, better shelter, more luxury, more beauty, more knowledge, more pleasure--increase in something, more life.

Every living thing is under this necessity for continuous advancement; where increase of life ceases, dissolution and death set in at once.

Man instinctively knows this, and hence he is forever seeking more. This law of perpetual increase is set forth by Jesus in the parable of the talents; only those who gain more retain any; from Him who hath not shall be taken away even that which he hath.

The normal desire for increased wealth is not an evil or a reprehensible thing; it is simply the desire for more abundant life; it is aspiration.

And because it is the deepest instinct of their natures, all men and women are attracted to him who can give them more of the means of life.

In following the Certain Way as described in the foregoing pages, you are getting continuous increase for yourself, and you are giving it to all with whom you deal.

You are a creative center, from which increase is given off to all.

Be sure of this, and convey assurance of the fact to every man, woman, and child with whom you come in contact. No matter how small the transaction, even if it be only the selling of a stick of candy to a little child, put into it the thought of increase, and make sure that the customer is impressed with the thought.

Convey the impression of advancement with everything you do, so that all people shall receive the impression that you are an Advancing Man, and that you advance all who deal with you. Even to the people whom you meet in a social way, without any thought of business, and to whom you do not try to sell anything, give the thought of increase.

You can convey this impression by holding the unshakable faith that you, yourself, are in the Way of Increase; and by letting this faith inspire, fill, and permeate every action.

Do everything that you do in the firm conviction that you are an advancing personality, and that you are giving advancement to everybody.

Feel that you are getting rich, and that in so doing you are making others rich, and conferring benefits on all.

Do not boast or brag of your success, or talk about it unnecessarily; true faith is never boastful.

Wherever you find a boastful person, you find one who is secretly doubtful and afraid. Simply feel the faith, and let it work out in every transaction; let every act and tone and look express the quiet assurance that you are getting rich; that you are already rich. Words will not be necessary to communicate this feeling to others; they will feel the sense of increase when in your presence, and will be attracted to you again.

You must so impress others that they will feel that in associating with you they will get increase for themselves. See that you give them a use value greater than the cash value you are taking from them.

Take an honest pride in doing this, and let everybody know it; and you will have no lack of customers. People will go where they are given increase; and the Supreme, which desires increase in all, and which knows all, will move toward you men and women who have never heard of you. Your business will increase rapidly, and you will be surprised at the unexpected benefits which will come to you. You will be able from day to day to make larger combinations, secure greater advantages, and to go on into a more congenial vocation if you desire to do so.

But, in doing all this, you must never lose sight of your vision of what you want, or your faith and purpose to get what you want.

Let me here give you another word of caution in regard to motives.

Beware of the insidious temptation to seek for power over other men.

Nothing is so peasant to the unformed or partially developed mind as the exercise of power or dominion over others. The desire to rule for selfish gratification has been the curse of the world. For countless ages kings and lords have drenched the earth with blood in their battles to extend their dominions; this not to seek more life for all, but to get more power for themselves.

Today, the main motive in the business and industrial world is the same; men marshal their armies of dollars, and lay waste the lives and hearts of millions in the same mad scramble for power over others. Commercial kings, like political kings, are inspired by the lust for power.

Jesus saw in this desire for mastery the moving impulse of that evil world He sought to overthrow. Read the twenty-third chapter of Matthew, and see how He pictures the lust of the Pharisees to be called "Master," to sit in the high places, to domineer over others, and to lay burdens on the backs of the less fortunate; and not how He compares this lust for dominion with the brotherly seeking for the Common Good to which He calls His disciples.

Look out for the temptation to seek for authority, to become a "master," to be considered as one who is above the common herd, to impress others by lavish display, and so on.

The mind that seeks for mastery over others is the competitive mind; and the competitive mind is not the creative one. In order to master your environment and your destiny, it is not all necessary that you should rule over your fellow men and indeed, when you fall into the world's struggle for the high places, you begin to be conquered by fate and environment, and your getting rich becomes a matter of chance and speculation.

Beware of the competitive mind! No better statement of the principle of creative action can be formulated than the favorite declaration of the lat "Golden Rule" Jones of Toledo: "What I want for myself, I want for everybody."

CHAPTER FOURTEEN ½

TURN IT UP! GIVE ME MORE! WE ALL HAVE a very old instinct that drives human nature. That human nature is what drives everything that we do. It is the driving impulse for more life. It's hard to understand more life other than one's own. However, when you start to think about life's purpose and generations to come, you really clarify an increase with not only life, but the quality of life.

I like the ideas that were conveyed at the back of this chapter when it comes to increasing everything about life. I think when you are creative and expand life because of what you create and what you think about, you have truly hit a groove with the universe and some of the most beautiful things are created, when we feel one with the universe. Sometimes we call it Zen or Feng Shui .

Then you have another situation where the competitive mind takes over. It steals the very things that the creative mind produces. When the competitive mind takes over its fuel is ego. When ego is the fuel it is not an inexhaustible supply. It has to be fed all of the time. Showing off to feel better about what you have or what you have done is a game that is not long lasting. You can never keep up with the creative mind by being competitive.

I know people that are geared by the competitive mind. How? I used to be geared that way. I guess that athletics instills a lot of competitiveness in people. As I have gotten older, I would much rather be creative than competitive. It's a lot more entertaining and in the end you feel more complete. You will also feel more comfortable. The beginnings of our universe started with creation, not competition. The very grain of our soles is to create. Creating means to advance life; advancing life means to grow as a species. With a Biology background, I am often in conversations on topics about Charles Darwin and his theories of evolution. In his classic book, *The Origin of Species,* evolution seems to occur through classic competition. (Remember survival of the fittest?) I disagree slightly. Evolution occurs from the creativeness of the species to perpetuate life! (Is that deep or what?)

Create your life instead of competing for it! Are you creating the life you want?

CHAPTER FIFTEEN

♦THE ADVANCING MAN♦

WHAT I HAVE SAID IN THE LAST CHAPTER applies as well to the professional man and the wage-earner as to the man who is engaged in mercantile business.

No matter whether you are a physician, a teacher, or a clergyman, if you can give increase of life to others and make them sensible of the fact, they will be attracted to you, and you will get rich. The physician who holds the vision of himself as a great and successful healer, and who works toward the complete realization of that vision with faith and purpose; as described in former chapters, will come into such close touch with the Source of Life that he will be phenomenally successful; patients will come to him in throngs.

No one has a greater opportunity to carry into effect the teachings of this book than the practitioner of medicine; it does not matter to which of the various schools he may belong, for the principle of healing is common to all of them, and may be reached by all alike. The Advancing Man in medicine, who holds to a clear mental image of himself as a successful, and who obeys the laws of faith, purpose, and gratitude, will cure every curable case he undertakes, no matter what remedies he may use.

In the field of religion, the world cries out for the clergyman who can teach his hearers the true science of abundant life. He who masters the details of the science of getting rich, together with the allied sciences of being well, of being great, and of winning love, and who teaches these details from the pulpit, will never lack for a congregation, This is the gospel that the world needs; it will give increase of life, and men will hear it gladly, and will give liberal support to the man who brings it to them.

What is now needed is a demonstration of the science of life from the pulpit. We want preachers who can not only tell us how, but who in their own persons will show us how. We need the preacher who will himself be rich, healthy, great, and beloved, to teach us how to attain to these things; and when he comes he will find a numerous and loyal following.

The same is true of the teacher who can inspire the children with the faith and purpose of the advancing life. He will never be "out of a job." And any teacher who has this faith and purpose can give it to his pupils; he cannot help giving it to them if it is part of his own life and practice.

What is true of the teacher, preacher, and physician is true of the lawyer, dentist, real-estate man, insurance agent--of everybody.

The combined mental and personal action I have described is infallible; it cannot fail. Every man and woman who follows these instructions steadily, perseveringly, and to the letter, will get rich. The law of the Increase of Life is as mathematically certain in its operation as the law of gravitation; getting rich is an exact science.

The wage-earner will find this as true of his case as of any of the others mentioned. Do not fell that you have no chance to get rich because you are working where there is no visible opportunity for advancement, where wages are small and the cost of living high. Form your clear mental vision of what you want, and begin to act with faith and purpose.

Do all the work you can do, every day, and do each piece of work in a perfectly successful manner; put the power of success, and the purpose to get rich, into everything that you do.

But do not do this merely with the idea currying favor with your employer, in the hope that he, or those above you, will see your good work and advance you; it is not likely that they will do so.

The man who is merely a "good" workman, filling his place to the very best of his ability, and satisfied with that, is valuable to his employer; and it is not to the employer's interest to promote him; he is worth more where he is.

To secure advancement, something more is necessary than to be too large for your place.

The man who is certain to advance is the one who is too big for his place, and who has a clear concept of what he wants to be; who knows that he can become what he wants to be and who is determined to *be* what he wants to be.

Do not try to more than fill your present place with a view to pleasing your employer; do it with the idea of advancing yourself. Hold the faith and purpose of increase during work hours, after work hours, and before work hours. Hold it in such a way that every person who comes in contact with you, whether foreman, fellow workman, or social acquaintance, will feel the power of purpose radiating from you; so that everyone will get the sense of advancement and increase from you. Men will be attracted to you, and if there is no possibility for advancement in your present job, you will very soon see an opportunity to take another job.

There is a Power which never fails to present opportunity to the Advancing Man who is moving in obedience to law.

God cannot help helping you, if you act in a Certain Way; He must do so in order to help Himself.

There is nothing in your circumstances or in the industrial situation that can keep you down. If you cannot get rich working for the steel trust, you can get rich on a ten-acre farm; and if you begin to move in the Certain Way, you will certainly escape from the "clutches" of the steel trust and get on to the farm or wherever else you wish to be.

If a few thousands of its employees would enter upon the Certain Way, the steel trust would soon be in a bad plight; it would have to give its workingmen more opportunity, or go out of business. Nobody has to work for a trust; the trusts can keep men in so-called hopeless conditions only so long as there are men who are too ignorant to know of the science of getting rich, or too intellectually slothful to practice it.

Begin this way of thinking and acting, and your faith and purpose will make you quick to see any opportunity to better your condition.

Such opportunities will speedily come, for the Supreme, working in All, and working for you, will bring them before you.

Do not wait for an opportunity to be all that you want to be; when an opportunity to be more than you are now is presented and you feel impelled toward it, take it. It will be the first step toward a greater opportunity.

There is no such thing possible in this universe as a lack of opportunities for the man who is living the advancing life.

It is inherent in the constitution of the cosmos that all things shall be for him and work together for his good; and he must certainly get rich if he acts and thinks in the Certain Way. So let wage-earning men and woman study this book with great care, and enter with confidence upon the course of action it prescribes; it will not fail.

CHAPTER FIFTEEN ½

THE ADVANCING MAN AND HIS NEED IN society is great! I cannot tell you how many people that have no idea about what it takes to lead people. This chapter talks about a lot of people and their walks of life. Ministers, doctors and teachers are probably the most needed people in our society. Because of that, they are often the people that are mostly leading people down the wrong path.

How much better of people would we be if we all acted in this certain way as the book has talked about. If we start to live in such a way that we are creative instead of competitive, we may be able to finally live in a world of peace instead of war. We may find ways to eliminate poverty and disease. I think it's a wonderful opportunity that we have and it start and ends with you! Let's get started! It starts and ends with everyone. Isn't competition the very thing that starts wars? Competition for oil. Competition for land. Competition for religion. Do we really have the right to compete for those things in the first place? With competition we operate on the basis of security. Take oil for example. We compete for oil every day. We pay for it, we kill for it and we consume it. Wouldn't it be great if we could be more creative with our energy sources? Our environment, our economics and our value of life would all improve globally if we came together on the creative plane!

What can you create?

CHAPTER SIXTEEN

♦SOME CAUTIONS AND CONCLUDING OBSERVATIONS♦

MANY PEOPLE WILL SCOFF AT THE IDEA that there is an exact science of getting rich; holding the impression that the supply of wealth is limited, they will insist that social and governmental institutions must be changed before even any considerable number of people can acquire a competence.

But this is not true.

It is true that existing governments keep the masses in poverty, but this is because the masses do not think and act in the Certain Way.

If the masses begin to move forward as suggested in this book, neither governments not industrial systems can check them; all systems must be modified to accommodate the forward movement.

If the people have the Advancing Mind, have the Faith that they can become rich, and move forward with the fixed purpose to become rich, nothing can possibly keep them in poverty.

Individuals may enter upon the Certain Way at anytime, and under any government, and make themselves rich; and when any considerable number of individuals do so under any government, they will cause the system to be so modified as to open the way for others.

The more men who get rich on the competitive plane, the worse for others; the more who get rich on the creative plane, the better for others.

The economic salvation of the masses can only be accomplished by getting a large number of people to practice the scientific method set down in this book, and become rich. These will show others the way, and inspire them with a desire for real life, with the faith that it can be attained, and with the purpose to attain it.

For the present, however, it is enough to know that neither the government under which you live nor the capitalistic or competitive system of industry can keep you from getting rich. When you enter upon the creative plane of thought you will rise above all these things and become a citizen of another kingdom.

But remember that your thought must be held upon the creative plane; you are never for an instant to be betrayed in to regarding the supply as limited, or into acting on the moral level of competition.

Whenever you do fall into old ways of thought, correct yourself instantly; for when you are in the competitive mind, you have lost the cooperation of the Mind of the Whole.

Do not spend any time in planning as to how you will meet possible emergencies in the future, except as the necessary policies may affect your actions today. You are concerned with doing today's work in a perfectly successful manner, and not with emergencies which may arise tomorrow; you can attend to them as they come.

Do not concern yourself with questions as to how you shall surmount obstacles which may loom upon your business horizon, unless you can see plainly that your course must be altered today in order to avoid them.

No matter how tremendous an obstruction may appear at a distance, you will find that if you go on in the Certain Way it will disappear as you approach it, or that a way over, through, or around it will appear.

No possible combination of circumstances can defeat a man or woman who is proceeding to get rich along strictly scientific lines. No man or woman who obeys the law can fail to get rich, anymore than the one can multiply two by two and fail to get four.

Give no anxious thought to possible disasters, obstacles, panics, or unfavorable combinations of circumstances; it is time enough to meet such things when they present themselves before you in the immediate present, and you will find that every difficulty carries with it the wherewithal for its overcoming.

Guard your speech. Never speak of yourself, your affairs, or of anything else in a discouraged or discouraging way.

Never admit the possibility of failure, or speak in a way that infers failure as a possibility.

Never speak of the times as being hard, or of business conditions as being doubtful. Times may be hard and business doubtful for those who are on the competitive plane, but they can never be so for you; you can create what you want, and you are above fear.

When others are having hard times and poor business, you will find your greatest opportunities.

Train yourself to think of and to look upon the world as a something which is Becoming, which is growing; and to regard seeming evil as being only that which is undeveloped. Always speak in terms of advancement; to do otherwise is to deny your faith, and to deny your faith is to lose it.

Never allow yourself to feel disappointed. You may expect to have a certain thing at a certain time, and not get it at that time; and this will appear to you like failure.

But if you hold to your faith you will find that the failure is only apparent.

Go on in the Certain Way, and if you do not receive that thing, you will receive something so much better that you will see that the seeming failure was really a great success.

A student of this science had set his mind on making a certain business combination which seemed to him at the time to be very desirable, and he worked for some weeks to bring it about.

When the crucial time came, the thing failed in a perfectly inexplicable way, it was as if some unseen influence had been working secretly against him. He was not disappointed; on the contrary, he thanked God that his desire had been overruled, and went steadily on with a grateful mind. In a few weeks an opportunity so much better came his way that he would not have made the first deal on any account; and he saw that a Mind which knew more than he knew had prevented him from losing the greater good by entangling himself with the lesser.

That is the way every seeming failure will work out for you, if you keep your faith, hold to your purpose, have gratitude, and do, every day, all that can be done that day, doing each separate act in a successful manner.

When you make a failure, it is because you have not asked for enough; keep on, and a larger thing than you were seeking will certainly come to you. Remember this.

You will not fail because you lack the necessary talent to do what you wish to do. If you go on as I have directed, you will develop all the talent that is necessary to the doing of your work.

It is not within the scope of this book to deal with the science of cultivating talent; but it is as certain and simple as the process of getting rich.

However, do not hesitate or waver for fear that when you come to any certain place you will fail for lack of ability; keep right on, and when you come to that place, the ability will be furnished to you. The same source of Ability which enabled the untaught Lincoln to do the greatest work in government ever accomplished by a single man is open to you; you may draw upon all the mind there is for wisdom to use in meeting the responsibilities which are laid upon you. Go on in full faith.

Study this book. Make it your constant companion until you have mastered all the ideas contained in it. While you are getting firmly established in this faith, you will do well to give up most recreations and pleasure; and to stay away from places where ideas conflicting with these are advanced in lectures or sermons. Do not read pessimistic or conflicting literature, or get into arguments upon the matter. Do very little reading, outside of the writers mentioned in the preface. Spend most of your leisure time in contemplating your vision, and in cultivating gratitude, and in reading this book. It contains all you need to know of the science of getting rich; and you will find all the essentials summed up in the following chapter.

CHAPTER SEVENTEEN

♦SUMMARY OF THE SCIENCE OF GETTING RICH♦

THERE IS A THINKING STUFF FROM WHICH all things are made, and which, in its original state, permeates, penetrates, and fills the interspaces of the universe.

A thought in this substance produces the thing that is imaged by the thought.

Man can form things in his thought, and by impressing his thought upon Formless Substance can cause the thing he thinks about to be created.

In order to do this, man must pass from the competitive to the creative mind; otherwise he cannot be in harmony with the Formless Intelligence, which is always creative and never competitive in spirit.

Man may come into full harmony with the Formless Substance by entertaining a lively and sincere gratitude for the blessings it bestows upon him. Gratitude unifies the mind of man with the intelligence of Substance, so that man's thought are received by the Formless. Man can remain upon the creative plane only by uniting himself with the Formless Intelligence through a deep and continuous feeling of gratitude.

Man must form a clear and definite mental image of the things he wishes to have, to do, or to become; and he must hold this mental image in his thoughts, while being deeply grateful to the Supreme that all his desires are granted to him. The man who wishes to get rich must spend his leisure hours in contemplating his Vision, and in earnest thanksgiving that the reality is being given to him. Too much stress cannot be laid on the importance of frequent contemplation of the mental image, coupled with unwavering faith and devout gratitude. This is the process by which the impression is given to the Formless, and the creative forces set in motion.

The creative energy works through the established channels of natural growth, and of the industrial and social order. All that is included in his mental image will surely be brought to the man who follows the instructions given above, and whose faith does not waver. What he wants will come to him through the ways of established trade and commerce.

In order to receive his own when it shall come to him, man must be active; and this activity can only consist in more than filling his present place. He must keep in mind the Purpose to get rich through the realization of his mental image. And he must do, every day, all that can be done that day, taking care to do each act in a successful manner. He must give to every man a use value in excess of the cash value he receives, so that each transaction makes for more life; and he must so hold the Advancing Thought that the impression of increase will be communicated to all with whom he comes in contact.

The men and women who practice the foregoing instructions will certainly get rich; AND THE RICHES THEY RE-

CEIVE WILL BE IN EXACT PROPORTION TO THE DEFINITENESS OF THEIR VISION, THE FIXITY OF THEIR PURPOSE, THE STEADINESS OF THEIR FAITH, AND THE DEPTH OF THEIR GRATITUDE.

THE END

CHAPTER SIXTEEN ½

CHAPTER SEVENTEEN ½

I THINK WALLACE WATTLES SUMMED UP the book very well in the last two chapters. At this time I recommend reading the last two chapters again. They say it all!

The conclusion of this book (or really two books in one) should have unlocked a secret for you. I think it has to do with what everyone searches for: happiness. The secret that this book unlocks is that *The Science of Getting Rich* and *The Alchemy of Wealth* have nothing to do with money!

As I have delivered lectures and spoke all over the world, I have noticed some things about happiness. Most people that are unhappy about where they are in life, probably has to do with where they seek happiness. It seems like they try to obtain happiness from external sources. Money or the lack of it usually plays a role unfortunately. STOP making money your leader!

Learn to find happiness internally. If you can create that from internal sources you will have an inexhaustible fuel of satisfaction in life. Remember two things: One, Money is geared by ego. Have you seen people geared by ego? They are short lived. Two, finding happiness internally gives you the opportunity to explore the true joys in life…love, nature and spirituality, to name a few. Money has nothing to do with those.

The Science of Getting Rich and *The Alchemy of Wealth* have to do with life and the advancement of it. We are all organisms in this universe and believe me, the pursuit of money is not what we are after. Our creator's purpose for us is not to obtain money. The purpose is to obtain life! You have arrived!

I want to wish you sincere success with your life! I have faith in you! Please keep me in mind during your journey as I have you in my thoughts daily!

Congratulations on what you're about to achieve.

Johnny D.

♦Books by John Dessauer♦

The Alchemy of Wealth
Give copies to family, friends, and co-workers…

Hardcover copy
$24.95
(Dessauer Publishing 2009)
Available at www.Amazon.com

Real Estate H20
A must read for anyone who is interested in Real Estate Investing. Drink it Up!

Hardcover copy
$24.95
(Dessauer Publishing, 2008)
Available at
www.Amazon.com